The Protection of Fundamental Rights
in the Legal Order of the European Union

Manfred A. Dauses

The Protection of Fundamental Rights in the Legal Order of the European Union

With Emphasis on the Institutional Protection of those Rights

PETER LANG
Frankfurt am Main · Berlin · Bern · Bruxelles · New York · Oxford · Wien

Bibliographic Information published by the Deutsche Nationalbibliothek
The Deutsche Nationalbibliothek lists this publication in the Deutsche Nationalbibliografie; detailed bibliographic data is available in the internet at http://dnb.d-nb.de.

Cover Design:
Olaf Glöckler, Atelier Platen, Friedberg

ISBN 978-3-631-60418-2

www.peterlang.de

Preface

The composition of this study took place during an eventful and turbulent period in terms of European fundamental rights. After about four decades of gradual development of a Community fundamental rights doctrine by an increasingly problem-oriented casuistry of the European Court of Justice (ECJ), the way to a fundamental rights codification at the Community/Union level was paved for the first time with the adoption of the Charter of Fundamental Rights of the European Union on 7 December 2000, which today embodies the key substance of the European *acquis* in the area of fundamental rights.

Initially, this Charter was adopted as a mere solemn proclamation, without a direct legally binding effect, although the unanimous intention of all the political powers involved aimed, from the very beginning, to shape the Charter in such a manner that the finality of a smooth integration in the primary law of the Union was kept in view. In doing so, the Treaty establishing a Constitution for Europe (of 29 October 2004), which was in preparation at that time, was thought of first of all, in which the Charter of Fundamental Rights should be inserted as Chapter II. After the failure of the ambitious constitutional plans as a result of the negative outcome of the referendums in France and the Netherlands, the efforts then concentrated on structurally linking the Charter of Fundamental Rights to the Lisbon Reform Treaty (of 13 December 2007), which was conceived as the successor to the Treaty establishing a Constitution for Europe. The link should take the form of a cross-reference in the Lisbon Reform Treaty, drawing attention to that the Charter of Fundamental Rights shall be legally binding and have the same legal value as the Treaties (Art. 6(1) 1st sentence TEU, new version).

On the basis of the law-making judicature of the ECJ, the first main part of the present paper traces the aforementioned developments, so as to subsequently address the second focal point, the institutional protection of fundamental rights, i.e., the system of legal protection in the Community/Union and its effects on the substantive protection of fundamental rights. In this context, in particular, the question has been examined whether the existing means of actions and judgements are suitable to guarantee an efficient protection of fundamental rights in the Community/Union legal order, or whether they require modification and, if need be, whether the method of a mere adaptation or expansion of the applicable provisions for legal protection or rather a substantive supplementation of these provisions, for instance, by introducing a specific Union fundamental rights complaint, should be aspired. In conclusion, an adaptation of the existing instruments for the protection of fundamental rights to the legitimate need of the fundamental rights-holders is favoured. On the other hand, the creation of a specific fundamental rights complaint as a new, additional procedural instrument with subsidiary character is deemed to be unnecessary.

The present study is a translation of the original German study "*Der Schutz der Grundrechte in der Rechtsordnung der Europäischen Union, unter besonderer Berücksichtigung des institutionellen Schutzes dieser Rechte*" (Peter Lang, 2010, 175 pages). Thereby, however, consideration was given to the fact that, in the meantime, the Lisbon Reform Treaty has entered into force on 1 December 2009.

Mr. Mohit Sehdev, New Delhi, was in charge of the translation and revision work. The author is full of praise for Mr. Sehdev, and expresses his sincere thanks for Mr. Sehdev's professional cooperation in the realisation of the English text version.

Bamberg, 2010 Prof. Dr. Dr. Dr. h.c. mult. Manfred A. Dauses

Table of Contents

Contents

List of abbreviations

AöR	Archiv des öffentlichen Rechts [Journal – Archive of Public Law]
BVerfG	Bundesverfassungsgericht [German Federal Constitutional Court]
BVerfGE	Collection of decisions of the Federal Constitutional Court
cf.	Compare (*Latin*: confer)
CFI	Court of First Instance of the European Communities
DÖV	Die Öffentliche Verwaltung [Public Administration (Journal)]
DVBl	Deutsches Verwaltungsblatt [German Administrative Journal]
e.g.	For example
EC	European Community/Communities
EC Treaty	Treaty establishing the European Community (name of the EEC Treaty in the version of Maastricht Treaty on European Union)
ECHR	European Convention on Human Rights
ECJ	Court of Justice of the European Communities /Court of Justice of the European Union / European Court of Justice
ECR	European Court Records (from 1990: Part I of the official records)
ECSC	European Coal and Steel Community
ECSC Treaty	Treaty establishing the Coal and Steel Community
ECtHR	European Court of Human Rights
EEC	European Economic Community
EEC Treaty	Treaty establishing the European Economic Community
ELR	European Law Review [Journal]
EP/PE	European Parliament
et seq.	and the following one [*Latin*: et sequens]
et seqq.	and those following [*Latin*: et sequentes]
etc.	et cetera
EU	European Union
EU Treaty	Treaty on European Union

EuGE	Collection of decisions of the Court of First Instance of the European Communities (Part II of the official records)
EuGRZ	Europäische Grundrechte [Journal – European Fundamental Rights]
EuR	Europarecht [Journal – European Law]
Euratom	European Atomic Energy Community
Euratom Treaty	Treaty establishing the European Atomic Energy Community
EuZW	Europäische Zeitschrift für Wirtschaftsrecht [European Journal of Business Law]
GC	General Court of the European Union
GG	Grundgesetz [German Basic Law]
Hrsg.	Publisher/Editor
i.e.	that is [*Latin*: id est]
ibid.	In the same place
ibidem	In the same place
JÖR	Jahrbuch des Öffentlichen Rechts der Gegenwart [Yearbook of Modern Public Law]
JuS	Juristische Schulung [Periodical – Legal Training]
JZ	Juristenzeitung [Law Journal]
NJW	Neue Juristische Wochenschrift [German Law Journal]
No.	Number
NVwZ	Neue Zeitschrift für Verwaltungsrecht [New Journal for Administrative Law]
OJ.	Official Journal of the European Communities
OSCE	Organisation for Security and Co-operation in Europe
p.	Page
SJZ	Schweizerische Juristenzeitung [Swiss Law Journal]
TEC	Treaty establishing the European Community (name of the EEC Treaty in the version of Maastricht Treaty on European Union)
TEU	Treaty on European Union
TFEU	Treaty on the Functioning of the European Union
UNTS	United Nations Treaty Series
viz.	that is to say [*Latin*: Videlicet]
vol.	Volume
v/vs.	versus
ZEuS	Zeitschrift für europarechtliche Studien [Journal for European Law Studies]
ZRP	Zeitschrift für Rechtspolitik [Journal of Law and Policy]

1. Introduction: The importance of international fundamental rights in today's world

The protection of fundamental rights in the legal order of the European Communities/European Union has long been a subject of just as lively and as critical discussion. The following reasons may be responsible for the growing awareness of the fundamental rights:

First, the alarming increase in intolerance, persecution and violence, which causes the political conflicts in vast regions of the world, has increased the awareness for providing fundamental rights and human rights protection. The "Charter for a New Europe", which was adopted on 21.11.1990 in Paris by the Heads of State and Government of the Conference for Security and Cooperation in Europe, makes it quite clear: "Human rights and fundamental freedoms are the birthright of all human beings, are inalienable and are guaranteed by law. Their protection and promotion is the first responsibility of government. Respect for them is an essential safeguard against an overmighty State. Their observance and full exercise are the foundation of freedom, justice and peace."

Another reason for the high topicality of the discussion on fundamental rights may be sought in the close connection of the problem with the demand for the rule of law and democracy. Europe is in a state of profound social and political flux. The decade-long cherished hopes and expectations of all the European people for democratic regimes, which are committed to human rights and fundamental freedoms, now seem to come true. The "Charter for European Security" of the OSCE, adopted in Istanbul on 19.11.1999, states that "The Heads of State or Government of the participating States ... reaffirm that respect for human rights and fundamental freedoms, democracy and the rule of law is at the core of OSCE's comprehensive concept of security" (Point 19 of the Charter)".

A third point concerns the shift in the understanding of fundamental rights in modern society. In the classic fundamental rights catalogues of the constitutions, the liberal fundamental and human rights, such as the protection of personal freedom against governmental paternalism and regimentation were prominent, and today, the fundamental social rights, such as the right to work, social security, education and culture are increasingly taking the center stage. Their function consists not so much in securing the individual spaces of freedom, but rather in justifying the rights to benefit from the State and society, social rights of codetermination and participation.

Particular attention is paid to the issue of fundamental rights within the scope of the legal order of the European Communities/European Union. Traditionally, the fundamental rights are an attribute of the States. The EC/EU is (still) not generally believed to be a polity, but a supranational organisation emerged from a functionally limited association of sovereign States. It does not have the three classic elements of statehood, viz., national territory, constitutive people and State power[1]: Its territory is the aggregate of the territories of the Member States, and its territorial borders coincide with their external borders; its population is the totality of the people of the Member States. The sovereign power exercised by it is not original, but results from the partial transfer of sovereign rights by the Member States of the EC/EU.

Nevertheless, the EC/EU already possesses state-like characteristics; it exercises quasi state-like power, which is, above all, reflected in the following central aspects: It has its own autonomous legal order, which intrinsically differentiates it from the legal order established by the general international agreements; its provisions can have direct effect, and in fact, not only vis-à-vis those Member States, which constituted them, but also vis-à-vis the individuals[2], and they enjoy primacy over any national law.[3] In view of these specificities of the Community/Union Law, the principle of the *rule of law* demands that the EC/EU respects and protects the fundamental rights in a similar manner as a polity.

---

1 According to the famous "Allgemeine Staatslehre" [General Theory of the State] by Georg Jellinek, 3rd edition, 1914, reprint 1966, p. 394 et seqq..

2 Judgement of 5.2.1963, van Gend & Loos, Case 26/62, ECR 1963, 1.

3 Judgement of 15.7.1964, Costa v E.N.E.L., Case 6/64, ECR 1964, 1251.

2. The historic deficit of comprehensive guarantees of fundamental rights in the written Community/Union Law

2.1. The historic lacunas in the "lex scripta" on fundamental rights

As is generally known, the protection of fundamental rights of the individual is strongly enshrined in the constitutional orders, which look back on a long tradition, of all the Member States of the European Union. The majority of the Member States commit themselves to the guarantees of elementary human and fundamental rights, which are listed in the form of a catalogue in their written constitutions. The United Kingdom and France earmark a special formal situation.

The United Kingdom, which, for lack of a formal constitutional concept, is unaware of a dogmatic fundamental rights concept, implicitly recognises certain "fundamental liberties" and "civil rights" in the literature and judicature as the component of its democratic-constitutional self-image. The French Constitution of the 5th Republic of 1958 waives the enumeration of individual fundamental rights, however, refers in its opening remarks to the historic Declaration of Human and Civil Rights of 1789, and to their affirmation in the preamble to the Constitution of the 4th Republic of 1946.

It is common to all the EU Member States, without exception, that they belong to the Convention for the Protection of Human Rights and Fundamental Freedoms of 4.11.1950 (European Convention on Human Rights, ECHR)[4].

On the other hand, till the adoption of the Charter of Fundamental Rights of the European Union on 7.12.2000[5], the European Community/Union had not seen any self-contained catalogue of fundamental rights, which would have been comparable to the fundamental rights component of a democratic constitution under the rule of law.[6] Also, neither the Community nor the Union are contracting parties to the ECHR. The long-cherished intention to remedy the existing deficiency in a

4 International source: UNTS, vol.213, p. 221.

5 OJ. 2000, C 364/1.

6 Although the European Charter of Fundamental Rights, by virtue of its intention and contents, constitutes a complete enumeration of the fundamental rights applicable in the Union, however, irrespective of its high symbolic value, it has a legally binding effect only since the entry into force of the Lisbon Reform Treaty on 1.12.2009. Article 6(1)

catalogue of fundamental rights by way of an accession of the Community/Union to the ECHR, could not be realised to this day.[7]

However, these findings do not rule out that individual provisions of the Treaties, in particular, those with regard to the internal market freedoms, equal rights (prohibitions on discrimination) and the European citizenship, are accorded substantive human rights content.

The freedoms explicitly mentioned in the Treaties result, on the one hand, from the internal market concept, (" …an area without internal frontiers in which the free movement of goods, persons, services and capital is ensured", Article 26(2) TFEU; ex-Article 14(2) TEC), and, on the other hand, from the Union civil rights, which, irrespective of an occupation, include the right of the European citizens "to move and reside freely within the territory of the Member States" (Article 21(1) TFEU; ex-Article 18(1) TEC). The personal rights to freedom of movement exhibit the closest connection to the fundamental rights.

Specificities of prohibition on discrimination can be found, e.g., in:

- Article 40(2) TFEU (ex-Article 34(2) TEC): prohibition on any discrimination between producers or consumers in the area of the common organisation of agricultural markets;

- Article 45(2) TFEU (ex-Article 39(2) TEC: abolition of any discrimination based on nationality between workers of the Member States as regards the freedom of movement;
- Articles 49(2), 57(3) TFEU (ex-Articles 43(2) TEC, 50(3) TEC): taking-up and pursuit of activities as self-employed persons or the provision of cross-border services according to the provisions of the host State "for its own nationals";
- Article 110 TFEU (ex-Article 90 TEC): prohibition of discriminatory or protectionist internal taxation);

TEU (new version) refers to the Charter as a legally binding document (see Point 5 below).

7 After the ECJ decided in its opinion of 28.3.1996 ("accession of the Community to the Convention for the Protection of Human Rights and Fundamental Freedoms") that without an amendment of the institutional structure of legal protection under the Treaties, an accession of the EC to the ECHR will be inadmissible (Opinion 2/94, ECR 1996, I-1759), the legal obstacles for such an accession can be cleared only by Article 6(2) TEU in the version of Lisbon Reform Treaty. The Union was asked to accede to the ECHR along with the aforementioned provision.

- Article 157 TFEU (ex-Article 141 TEC): principle of equal pay for male and female workers for equal work or work of equal value.[8]

In addition, the EC/EU Treaties envisage three general groups of prohibitions on discrimination, which are applicable irrespective of the special provisions of the Treaties:

- Article 3(3.2) TEU (ex-Article 2 TEC): general principle of equality for women and men;
- Article 18 TFEU (ex-Article 12 TEC): prohibition of any discrimination on grounds of nationality within the scope of application of the Treaties;
- Article 19 TFEU (ex-Article 13 TEC): prohibition of "discrimination based on sex, racial or ethnic origin, religion or belief, disability, age or sexual orientation". However, this latter provision is not immediately applicable, but rather enables the Union legislator to take appropriate action, within the limits of the Union's powers to combat such discriminations.[9]

As another category of fundamental rights-related provisions of the EC Treaty, the signs of the democratic principles in the provisions on the citizenship of the Union are pointed out:

- Article 22(1) TFEU (ex-Article 19(1) TEC: participation of citizens of the Union in local elections in their State of residence;
- Article 22(2) TFEU (ex-Article 19(2) TEC): participation of all citizens of the Union to the elections to the European Parliament in their State of residence;
- Article 24 TFEU (ex-Article 21 TEC): Union citizens' right to petition the European Parliament, the Ombudsman, and the institutions and bodies of the European Union.

---

8 Article 141 (ex-Article 119) TEC was concretised by the Directive 75/117/EEC of 10.2.1975 (OJ. 1975, L 45/19), as amended by the Directive 2006/54/EC of 5.7.2006 (OJ. 2006, L 204/23). Several other labour law directives contain prohibitions on discrimination in the area of the primary law provision of Article 141 TEC. Of these, the most important is the Directive 76/207/EEC of 9.2.1976 on the implementation of the principle of equal treatment for men and women as regards access to employment, vocational training and promotion, as well as working conditions (OJ. 1976, L 39/40), as amended by the Directive 2002/73/EC of 23.9.2002 (OJ. 2002, L 269/15), as amended by the Directive 2006/54/EC of 5.7.2006, ibid.

9 Article 13 TEC forms the legal basis of the anti-discrimination Directives 2000/43/EC of 29.6.2000 (OJ. 2000, L 180/22), 2000/78/EC of 27.11.2000 (OJ. 2000, L 303/16), 2002/73/EC of 23.9.2002 (OJ. 2002, L 269/15) and 2004/113/EC of 13.12.2004 (OJ. 2004, L 373/37).

If, consequently, the Community/Union Treaties enshrine individually specific fundamental rights-relevant provisions from the outset, the fact that these texts are silent with regard to the comprehensive fundamental rights contents is, nevertheless, evident. The simple explanation can be found in the history of the Community/Union, which was originally conceived as a mere specialist organisation. Initially, the economic and technical character of the European Coal and Steel Community (ECSC), founded in 1951, was in the foreground, which made the vitiations of the fundamental value positions by the Community authorities look less realistic. When the European Economic Community (EEC) and European Atomic Energy Community (Euratom) were founded by the Treaties of Rome of 1957, the experience of the political failure came along as a political factor. The wide-spread plans for a European Defence Community (EDC) and a European (political) Community failed; the initial euphoria gave way to a down-to-earth utilitarianism, and obstructed the view on the universal idea of fundamental and human rights. A constitutional necessity for a communitarian catalogue of fundamental rights was not seen against this background.[10]

It was only with the Maastricht Treaty of 7.2.1992 that the non-economic functions and competences were incorporated on a large-scale into the newly established three-pillar-structure of the European Union. The shift of emphasis from the mere concept of an integrated economic area to a single legal area nurtured the demand for fundamental protection of individuals. As a significant progress, in the new Union Treaty, a general commitment to fundamental rights was incorporated, which in substance and wording follows the case-law of the European Court of Justice (ECJ), which was developed in the meantime (Article 6(2) TEU; cf. Article 6(3) TEU, new version):

"The Union shall respect fundamental rights, as guaranteed by the European Convention for the Protection of Human Rights and Fundamental Freedoms signed in Rome on 4 November 1950 and as they result from the constitutional traditions common to the Member States, as general principles of Community law."

This passage makes it clear that that the European Union shall respect the fundamental rights and, at the same time, clarifies the sources of law from which the fundamental rights of the Union flow: These are applicable as unwritten general principles of the Community law, the substance and scope of which arise from the European Convention on Human Rights and the constitutional traditions of the

10 This opinion was also represented, first of all, by the ECJ, which, in 1960, in the "Präsident" case, categorically negated the existence of European fundamental rights: judgement of 15.7.1960, Präsident, Cases 36/59, 37/59, 38/59 and 40/59, ECR 1960, 887, 920 et seq.

Member States. In other words, the fundamental rights are an integral component of the general principles of the Community law; they form the primary source of law for the fundamental rights. The European Convention on Human Rights, on the one hand, and the constitutional traditions common to the Member States, on the other hand, have to be referred to as the sources of the knowledge of law (secondary sources of law) for defining their substance.

However, even the Maastricht Treaty lacks a comprehensive catalogue of specified individual fundamental rights.

2.2. The requirement of a comprehensive praetorian protection of fundamental rights

The discussion on the lack of explicit and comprehensive fundamental rights guarantees in the Treaties, castigated by the representatives of the literature as "fundamental rights indifference"[11], has quite clearly shown that the protection of fundamental rights in the European Community in no way represents a marginal problem. The dangers due to the lack of a commitment to and penetration of the fundamental rights are apparent. They increase to the extent of the progressing integration of the individual in the social fabric of a technological mass society.

It's almost recognised as an axiomatic principle of the rule of law that the transfer of sovereign powers to the Community by disintegrating them from the national sovereignty may not lead to an impairment of the fundamental rights that are guaranteed by the national constitutional orders. According to that, the sovereign powers may be transferred only to the Community – with regard to the Federal Republic of Germany, on the basis of the constitutional law, Article 23(1) Basic Law (GG), formerly Article 24(1) GG –, if a protection of fundamental rights is guaranteed, which is adequate and, at least, in line with the national standards. The demand for congruence in the sphere of fundamental rights is again revealed as a specific form of expression of the further-reaching general demand for structural homogeneity, at least, however, structural congruence in the relationship of the Community legal order with the liberal and democratic legal orders of the Member States.

Therefore, the essence of the fundamental rights' issue under the Community law exists in ensuring that, irrespective of the much criticised lack of a fundamental rights catalogue in the Treaties, the communitarian protection of fundamental

11 Hans Peter Ipsen, Europäisches Gemeinschaftsrecht 1972, p. 723; idem, Der deutsche Jurist und das Europäische Gemeinschaftsrecht, Verhandlungen des 45. Deutschen Juristentages, Karlsruhe 1964, vol. II, p. L 1, L 15.

rights does not fall short of the democratic constitutional orders of the Member States. Accomplishment of this task was left to the law-making judicature of the European Court of Justice (ECJ), which, on the basis of the democratic and constitutional traditions common to the Member States and the conventions for the protection of human rights concluded by them, protects the fundamental rights as general principles of the Community law.

3. Dogmatic foundations of the fundamental rights' case-law of the ECJ

3.1. The emergence of fundamental rights' case-law of the ECJ

Consequently, the ascertainment and binding stipulation of the communitarian fundamental rights as general principles of law primarily devolves upon the ECJ within the scope of its function as the guardian of Community law. This process takes place over an evaluative comparison of law. This means that the Court of Justice grasps the standards from the different sources of the knowledge of law in an overall evaluative perspective, and seeks to harmonise the same with the objectives of the Community.[12]

Without having to deal with the details of the underlying facts, four basic judgements are pointed out by which the essential dogmatic foundations of the praetorian protection of fundamental rights were laid:

- The relevant case-law was introduced with the judgement of 12.11.1969 in the Stauder[13] case. In the said case, the ECJ had, using the concise phrase that "the provision at issue contains nothing capable of prejudicing the fundamental human rights enshrined in the general principles of the Community law and protected by the Court", counted the fundamental rights among the general fundamental principles of the Community legal order and, at the same time, affirmed its jurisdiction for the protection of these rights.
- The validity of the fundamental rights in the Community legal order and its relationship with the national fundamental rights guarantees were the focus

12 Hans-Werner Rengeling/Peter Szczekalla, Grundrechte in der Europäischen Union – Charta der Grundrechte und allgemeine Rechtsgrundsätze, 2004, p. 95; Ingolf Pernice, Grundrechtsgehalte im europäischen Gemeinschaftsrecht, Ein Beitrag zum gemeinschaftsimmanenten Grundrechtsschutz durch den Europäischen Gerichtshof, 1979, p. 135; Dieter Feger, Die Normsetzung auf dem Gebiet der Grundrechte in den Europäischen Gemeinschaften – Der Europäische Gerichtshof (EuGH) als Rechtsetzungsorgan, in: DÖV 1987, p. 322. See also: Pierre Pescatore, Bestand und Bedeutung der Grundrechte im Recht der Europäischen Gemeinschaften, in: EuR 1979, p. 1.

13 Case 29/69 ECR, 1969, 419.

of the Judgment of 17.12.1970 (Internationale Handelsgesellschaft).[14] In this verdict, the ECJ, contrary to the opinion of the referring court, refused to assess the fundamental rights compatibility of the secondary Community law by directly applying the national constitutional law, however, confirmed the existence of general principles of law for the protection of fundamental rights in the Community legal order, and further elaborated that the guarantee of these rights must be born by the constitutional traditions common to the Member States, however, must also fit in the structure and objectives of the Community. By using this phrase, the ECJ recognised the autonomous sources of law, and the autonomous validity of the protection of fundamental rights from the acts of the Community authorities, however, admitted that to ascertain these, the basic principles of the national legal orders should be referred to as the sources to find the law (*fontes cognoscendi*).

- In the judgements of 14.5.1974 (Nold)[15] and of 13.12.1979 (Hauer)[16], this case-law was further strengthened and consolidated. In the above judgements, the ECJ highlighted more clearly the relationship of the communitarian fundamental rights guarantees with the fundamental rights-related structural principles of the national constitutional orders. It underlined that it "cannot uphold any measures, which are incompatible with the fundamental rights recognised and protected by the constitutions [of the Member States]". Both the judgements are insightful also from another perspective that they have clarified the role of fundamental rights guarantees in international Treaties, in particular, the role of the Convention for the Protection of Human Rights and Fundamental Freedoms (ECHR) of 4.11.1950, which was ratified in the meantime by all the EU Member States. Although they did not accord a directly binding effect to the ECHR, however, recognised its important orientation role: " international Treaties for the protection of human rights, on which the Member States have collaborated or of which they are signatories, can supply guidelines, which should be followed within the framework of Community law". The doctrine, which has already been established in the judgement in the Internationale Handelsgesellschaft case, of immanent restrictions on fundamental rights was further expanded. The fundamental rights at issue (the judgement in Nold case concerned the rights freely to choose and practice the trade or profession, and the judgement in Hauer case concerned the right of ownership and the freedom to engage in trade or profession) are "far from constituting unfettered prerogatives", but must be "viewed in the light of the social function

14 Case 11/70, ECR 1970, 1125.
15 Case 4/73, ECR 1974, 491.
16 Case 44/79, ECR 1979, 3727.

of the property and activities protected thereunder". They allow interferences, which, however, are subject to restrictions on their part. These [restrictions] are especially clearly highlighted in the Hauer judgement on the values enshrined in the fundamental rights positions. They are of three types:

- justification of interference by the objectives serving the general interest of the Community,
- proportionality of interference with regard to the pursued objective,
- guarantee of the substance (essential content) of the protected right.

The emphasis of the initial case-law of the Court of Justice was naturally on the sources of law and the position of the fundamental rights in the overall structure of the Community law, while the substantive law definition of individual fundamental rights guarantees appeared little by little in the foreground. According to the predominant economic objectives of the Community, the fundamental rights guarantees, along with the economic and social reference, form the primary object of the initial case-law.

Interventions of the Community authorities in the right of ownership and the freedom to engage in business and to choose and practice a profession were the subject-matter of the cited judgements in the Internationale Handelsgesellschaft, Nold and Hauer cases. Using this example, the ECJ developed its doctrine of immanent restrictions on fundamental rights. In the judgements in the Internationale Handelsgesellschaft (provision of security within the scope of an export licensing system) and Nold cases (exclusion of a coal merchant from direct supply), these were identified rather indiscriminately as the dividing line between the legally protected assets and mere economic interests and prospects. In the judgement in Hauer case (prohibition on new planting of vines), these were paraphrased and defined with the help of the concept of general interest, the proportionality of the intervention and the – probably borrowed from the German constitutional case-law – guarantee of the substance (essential content).

3.2. Sources of law in the light of fundamental rights' case-law of the ECJ

As already described, according to Article 6(3) TEU (ex-Article 6(2) TEU), the fundamental rights in the Union are an integral part of the general principles of the Community law, for the determination of which the European Convention for the Protection of Human Rights and Fundamental Freedoms (ECHR), on the one hand, and the constitutional traditions common to the EU Member States, on the other hand, should be referred to as *fontes cognoscendi*.

3.2.1. Primary sources of law: the general principles of the Community law

The unwritten general principles of the Community law constitute the primary sources of law, from which the European Union's fundamental rights flow. These principles are – just as the provisions of the Community/Union Treaties – embodied in the system of gradation of norms as the primary law on top of the communitarian hierarchy of norms.[17] With the help of these principles, the existing gaps in the Community legal order could be plugged, and this legal order could be developed further to a harmonious, coherent overall system.[18]

The European Union's fundamental rights form a subcategory of the general principles of law, to which, in addition to the fundamental rights-related general phrases of the rule-of-law principle and procedural law (such as, e.g., requirements of legal certainty and protection of legitimate expectations, the principles of legality of administrative action and proportionality, as well as the general principles of criminal law "*nullum crimen sine lege*" and "*ne bis in idem*"), the general principles of law common to the legal orders of the Member States concerning the non-contractual liability of the Community/Union (Article 340(2) TFEU; ex-Article 288(2) TEC) should be assigned furthermore.

The literature has tried, on various occasions, to reach a terminological differentiation between the principles of law (*principes de droit*), which are non-binding and not directly obligatory, and the binding rules of law (*règles de droit*). According to this differentiation, the principles of law should represent pre- and extra-positive normative ideas, which flow from the general legal thinking, and which form the basis of the positive legal order, however, they themselves do not have a legislative character. They could justify the rights and duties of the legal subjects only insofar as they have been "adopted" by the legislative act or the law-making judgement. This terminological comparison, however, appears to be of little assistance for the interpretation of the fundamental rights jurisprudence of the ECJ. An analysis of the relevant case-law rather leads to the conclusion that the ECJ

---

17 This discovery results from the deliberation that the provisions of the Community/Union Treaties should be interpreted in the light of the unwritten general principles of the Community/Union law. Thus, for example, the restrictions on the market freedoms guaranteed in the EC Treaty (now: TFEU)could be justified by the requirements of the Member States' legal orders only if the restrictions are compatible with the fundamental rights and equivalent unwritten rights in the Community/Union legal order. See Udo Ostermann, Entwicklung und gegenwärtiger Stand der europäischen Grundrechte nach der Rechtsprechung des Europäischen Gerichtshofs sowie des Gerichts erster Instanz; this inaugural dissertation was supervised by the author of the present study at the Faculty of Law of the University of Erlangen-Nürnberg 2008, p. 12.

18 Cf. Gunter M. Hoffmann, Grundrechte in Europa – braucht Europa einen Grundrechtskatalog?, 1995, p. 20.

considers the general principles of law not as non-binding guiding legal principles, but as directly obligatory, operative norms, albeit of utmost generality and a high level of abstraction, which are enshrined in the general legal conscience, and from which the rights and obligations of the legal subjects can be inferred by judicial adjudication.

Quite logically, the principle of law and the legal norm are not in proportion to the antinomy, but are in a ratio of the subordinate concept to the superordinate concept, and, in fact, in the sense that not all legal norms, but only those based on the general legal thinking could be referred to as the principles of law. It is rightly pointed out that the particularity of the general principles of law does not consist in enabling none of the feasible solutions for the individual case, but rather in defining the fundamentals of the structure of the legal order and the principles of living together in a Community based on law with the consequence that a general principle of law could not be disregarded, unlike a "simple" rule of law, without questioning the fundamentals of the legal order itself.[19]

At the same time, this conclusion enables an answer to the question on the nature of the sources of the general principles of law. The reasoning of the Court of Justice unmistakably points towards that the general principles of law should be regarded as the primary source of law independent of the Treaties; it infers its legitimation, to refer to it for finding the law, from the legal thinking itself, which has found its most general expression in the Treaties, in the phrase that the Court of Justice ensures that the "law is observed" in the interpretation and application of the Treaties (Article 19(1) TEU; ex-Article 220(1) TEC).

The theory that the general principles of the Community law form a primary source of directly binding objective law is additionally confirmed by the overwhelming majority of opinions represented in the literature, whereupon the judicial legal activity is restricted to the mere ascertainment of the objective law, which is already assumed to be valid, by means of interpretation and by filling the gaps; thus the judicature is only the source of the knowledge of law, and not the original reason for the emergence of law. But this presupposes – at least, as a theoretical concept – that the general principles of law, which contain the fundamental rights, already possess a sufficient actuality so as to be applied to specific cases with the acknowledged methods of judicial hermeneutics.

In this context, the issue of hierarchical ranking of norms of the fundamental rights-related general principles of law in the structure of the Community/Union law needs to be mentioned once again. Undisputedly, these principles of law take

---

19 Cf. Helmut Lecheler, Der Europäische Gerichtshof und die allgemeinen Rechtsgrundsätze, 1971, p. 45 et seq.; see also: Theodor Schilling, Bestand und allgemeine Lehren der bürgerschützenden allgemeinen Rechtsgrundsätze des Gemeinschaftsrechts, in: EuGRZ 2000, p. 3 et seqq.

precedence over the secondary Community/Union law. This means that they should be cited as its assessment criteria with the consequence that the provisions of the secondary Community/Union law, which are incompatible with them, should be declared by the ECJ – depending on the type of proceeding – to be "void" (Article 264 TFEU; ex-Article 231 TEC), "invalid" (Article 267 TFEU; ex-Article 234 TEC) or "inapplicable" (Article 277 TFEU; ex-Article 241 TEC).

However, the issue of compatibility of primary Community/Union law with the fundamental rights guarantees has been found in none of the cases held before the ECJ until now, so that an authentic answer to the question of ranking between the general principles of law and the Community/Union Treaties cannot be given. However, it may be inherent in the reasoning of the existing case-law to grant priority ranking to the elementary principles of law, which are based upon universal legal thinking, as the foundation pillars of every Community or Union, at least, in the form of the prevalence of application; for it seems incompatible with their character as pre- and extra-positive juridico-ethical basic guarantees, if a positive law of any kind has priority over them.

3.2.2. Secondary sources of law: Member States' constitutional traditions and European Convention on Human Rights (ECHR)

3.2.2.1. Preliminary remark

The ascertainment that the fundamental rights in the Community/Union legal order are an integral part of the general principles of law indeed enshrines them dogmatically, however, does not specify the individual rights, and does not concretise their contents. In this regard, the secondary sources of law must be referred to (the sources of the knowledge of law: "*fontes cognoscendi*").

With regard to their effect, the latter differ from the primary sources of law in that they serve the ECJ only as a guidance in the derivation and contextual definition of the fundamental rights, but are not directly binding upon it. Article 6(3) TEU (ex-Article 6(2) TEU) explicitly identifies the ECHR, on the one hand, and the constitutional traditions common to the Member States, on the other hand, as the secondary sources of law. The Charter of Fundamental Rights of the European Union, which was solemnly proclaimed at the summit in Nice on 7.12.2000, was originally, prior to the coming into effect of the Lisbon Reform Treaty, conceived as an additional non-binding, secondary source of Community/Union law. By the Lisbon Treaty, however, it obtained the status of a directly binding legal instrument, which has the same legal value as the Treaties (Article 6(1) TEU, new version).

The following comments concentrate on the impact of the ECHR and the constitutional traditions common to the Member States as the characteristics of the communitarian protection of fundamental rights. The European Charter of Fundamental Rights will be discussed in detail below.[20]

Concerning the ranking of both the secondary sources of law mentioned in Article 6(3) TEU (ex-Article 6(2) TEU), the text of the Treaty considers them to be of equal rank, irrespective of the syntactic order in which they are listed. It is, in fact, conspicuous that the differentiating formula applied in the earlier judicature of the ECJ is not reflected in Article 6(3) TEU (ex-Article 6(2) TEU), whereupon the Court of Justice "cannot uphold measures, which are incompatible with the fundamental rights recognised and protected by the constitutions [of the Member States]", whereas "the international Treaties for the protection of human rights .... could supply guidelines, which should be followed within the framework of the Community law".[21]

Meanwhile, in the case-law of the ECJ, the ECHR plays a significantly larger role than the constitutional traditions common to the Member States, the similarities of which have been laid bare by the Court of Justice only in a few individual cases, by means of a comparative analysis. The reasons for this practical approach are comprehensible: The Convention influences the emergence of common European fundamental rights in a dual capacity, viz., as the reflection and summarisation of the fundamental rights-related national constitutional traditions, on the one hand, and as an independent secondary source of law, on the other hand.

Thus, the ECHR already reflects a fundamental consensus of the contracting parties to which all the EU Member States belong. Thereby, the Convention provides a basis of legitimation that is more sustainable than the individual constitutions of the Member States, with regard to which the ECJ has to work out, first of all, the common basic principles.[22]

The position and significance of the constitutional orders of the Member States and the ECHR in the structure of Community/Union law will be discussed hereafter.

3.2.2.2. Member States' constitutional traditions

The constitutional traditions common to the Member States reflect congruent legal conceptions and moral values of the States belonging to the communitarian circle of law. They are reflected in a general consensus via which the fundamental prin-

---

20 See below, statements on the European Charter of Fundamental Rights (Point 4).

21 Judgement of 14.5.1974, Nold, Case 4/73, ECR 1974, 491, 507; almost word for word judgement of 13.12.1979, Hauer, Case 44/79, ECR 1979, 3727, 3745.

22 Cf. Udo Ostermann, ibid., p. 23 et seqq., with numerous references.

ciples and basic structures of the national legal orders flow into the Community/ Union law.[23] Consequently, the key basis for the validity of the fundamental rights is rooted in the commonness of the constitutional bases of the Member States, the liberal and democratic principles of which the Community/Union is committed to as a "common solidary way of being of the Member States and their peoples".[24]

In this context, it seems appropriate to briefly summarise the criteria by which the ECJ was guided in defining and filling the gaps of the concept of "the constitutional traditions common to the Member States".

The Court proceeds on the assumption that in consideration of the European-wide different development of constitutional histories, which entails a different application of the concept and contents of fundamental rights, the national doctrines of fundamental rights cannot simply be "imposed" on the European law. A European fundamental rights doctrine can rather be developed only within the framework of the autonomous legal order of the European Union itself,[25] whereupon, the constitutional traditions of the Member States could only provide an informative basis within the meaning of a "common denominator" for a fundamental rights doctrine in Community/Union law.

With regard to the "commonality" of the constitutional traditions of the Member States, it is to be established that this should be determined by the ECJ by way of an evaluative comparison of laws. In doing so, it should be taken into consideration that the protection of fundamental rights in individual Member States is by no means uniform. Considerable differences arise even in case of fundamental rights, which are common to the constitutions of the Member States. These are to be attributed to the different understandings of fundamental rights, on the one hand, but, on the other hand, also to the diversified historical developments.[26] It becomes clear, above all, from the hierarchical classification of the fundamental rights in the national legal orders and from the missing conformity with the protective effect of the fundamental rights vis-à-vis the legislative rights. In many cases, it moreover proves to be unrealistic to include the legal orders of all the Member States in the judgemental comparison of law. Thus, the Court of Justice was, for instance, in the judgement in the "Hauer" case[27], content with proving

23 Hans Kutscher, Thesen zu den Methoden der Auslegung des Gemeinschaftsrechts aus der Sicht eines Richters, publication of the ECJ, Luxemburg 1976, p. I-8.

24 Pierre Pescatore, Bestand und Bedeutung der Grundrechte im Recht der Europäischen Gemeinschaften, in: EuR 1979, p. 1,5.

25 Cf. Hans-Werner Rengeling/Peter Szczekalla, Grundrechte in der Europäischen Union, ibid., p. 46.

26 Cf. Dirk Bornemann, Die Bedeutung der Grundrechtsquellen für den Grundrechtsschutz und die Grundrechtskollisionen in der Rechtsprechung des Europäischen Gerichtshofs, 2002, p. 86.

27 Judgement of 13. 12.1979, Case 44/79, EuGHE, ibid., 3745.

that a specific fundamental right – the right to property in that case – is guaranteed in selected constitutional orders of the Member States. It proceeded similarly in the "AM&S" case with regard to the right to confidentiality of the written communications between a lawyer and his client.[28] On the other hand, the ECJ, in the judgement in the "Hoechst" case,[29] due to the non-conformity of the national legal orders (12 at that time), denied the fundamental rights protection to the inviolability of the business premises.

In the judicial literature, in many cases, the so-called theory of maximum standards ("maximalist theory") is represented, i.e., the ECJ should, in case of different approaches in the individual Member States, preferably select that approach, which guarantees the highest level of protection of the fundamental rights.[30] A modified assumption results in a "negative control function" of the ECJ, which may in no case bring down the communitarian protection of fundamental rights to the point that the indispensable values of even a single national legal order are violated.[31]

The ECJ has not clearly recognised any of these theories in its case-law, rather administers justice pragmatically, having regard to all the circumstances of the specific case and by using a broad scope for judgement evaluation. In doing so, it in no way proceeds formalistically and schematically, and follows none of the rigid dogmatic rules. On the contrary, it endeavours, on a case-by-case basis, for the respective "optimum" outcome, i.e., the most reasonable and fairest solution, which, at the same time, best fits into the objectives and structures of the Community/Union.[32]

This approach of the Court of Justice should be accepted. The "evaluative" comparison of laws neither means that the mathematical "lowest common denominator" nor the maximum rule arising from the legal orders of the Member States should be searched for, and nor that it matters whether the general principles of law are verifiable in a majority of the Member States. The general principles of law do not develop one-dimensionally, but are defined by a plurality of factors.

---

28 So-called "*legal privilege*" of the Common Law: judgement of 18.5.1982, Case 155/79, ECR 1982, 1575. See further Point 3.6.5 below.

29 Judgement of 21.9.1989, Case 46/87 and 227/88, ECR 1989, 2859. See further Point 3.6.5 below.

30 Critical assessment thereof: Udo Ostermann, ibid., p. 32 et seq., with references.

31 Rudolf Streinz, Europarecht, 7th edition 2005, para 763.

32 With regard to the national legal orders, which are to be taken into consideration, the ECJ also focuses on the their weight and importance, a possible guiding role of some of these legal orders for the further development of the law in general, as well as on the political and economic weight of the Member States, which are behind the respective legal orders, cf. Gunter M. Hoffmann, ibid., p. 16 et seqq.

They should be subject to an overall assessment with regard to the objectives and structures of the Community/Union.

Finally, it is pointed out that not only the constitutional legal orders of the Member States contribute to the creation of common European constitutional traditions, and therewith, to the creation of general principles of Community/Union law, but also vice versa – through feedback – the common European constitutional traditions influence the national level of protection of fundamental rights in the Member States. Member States with a high level of protection, such as the Federal Republic of Germany, have to put up with long-term losses, whereas the Member States with a rather low standard of protection experience an expansion of their national protection of fundamental rights.

3.2.2.3. European Convention on Human Rights (ECHR)

Just as the Member States' constitutional traditions, the European Convention on Human Rights (ECHR), which was signed in Rome on 4.11.1950, and is in force since 3.7.1953, is a secondary, and not primary, source of the communitarian/Union's fundamental rights. Although all the (at present, 45) members of the European Council, and therewith all the EU Member States are parties to this Convention of States, however, the Community or the Union itself have not acceded to the ECHR until now, so that a formal commitment of the Community/Union is ruled out, in particular, the judicial system of the Convention cannot be engaged vis-à-vis the Community/Union. For this reason, a direct control of the Community legislation by the European Court of Human Rights is out of question.[33]

The ascertainment that the legal acts of the Community/Union are not directly subject to the jurisdiction of the European Court of Human Rights (ECtHR), however, leaves open the question whether or not an indirect supervisory power of this court over the Community/Union law, which is contrary to the Convention, should be assumed, that is to say, if the EU Member States implement this law,

33 In this connection, the European Commission on Human Rights, a former body of the ECHR, had decided, already on 10.7.1978, on a complaint of the French trade union CFDT (Confédération Française Démocratique du Travail [French Democratic Confederation of Labour]) against the European Communities, alternatively against the entirety of the EC Member States. The complainant had asserted that its rights enshrined in the ECHR had been violated in that it was not considered as a representative workers' trade union organisation in a decision of the Council of the EC. The Strasbourg Commission dismissed the complaint as inadmissible, in so far as it was directed against the European Communities, because they were not the parties to the Convention, and in so far as it was directed against the Member States, because they, by participating in the challenged decision, could not have exercised any jurisdiction within the meaning of the Convention: Application N°. 8030/77.

e.g., transpose directives into the national law or execute regulations administratively. In such a case, they have to accept the Community/Union law, which is possibly contrary to the Convention, substantively as their own legislative process. In this connection, the question whether the Convention States could, by transferring sovereign powers to the EC/EU, evade a supervision in the light of the Convention concluded by them, and therewith could evade their responsibilities under international law has been answered in the negative. The ECtHR had negated it. In this regard, it opined that the Convention States are, in the light of the Convention, under its supervision even if they act determinately as a community, thus, implement Community/Union law.[34]

A different problem kept the case-law of the ECJ occupied from the perspective of the European Community law. As has already been pointed out, indeed the ECJ does not consider the substantive provisions of the Convention as a directly integral part of the Community law, but rather as a source of the knowledge of law[35], whereupon, it defined the concept of the Convention to such an extent that it includes even the specific judgements of the European Court of Human Rights.[36]

The statement that the ECHR forms a secondary source of law of the fundamental rights in the Community/Union, however, does not exhaust the plethora of effects displayed by the international agreements of the Community or Union, as well as by such international agreements, which are on a par with them, and which were (still) concluded by the Member States, but refer to those subject-matters for which the jurisdiction has been passed on to the Community/Union in the meantime.

The Community/Union law knows no explicit provisions for the hierarchical ranking, in the Community/Union legal order, of the norms of the international agreements concluded by the Community or Union. However, useful references could be inferred from an established case-law of the ECJ. Accordingly, the international agreements of the Community are reckoned among the acts of the secondary communitarian law, but under this hierarchy of the norms of the EC/EU law,

---

34 European Commission of Human Rights, Decision of 9 February 1990, Melchers & Co v Federal Republic of Germany, Yearbook 1990, 46 (52); European Court of Human Rights, Judgment of 18 February 1999, Matthews v United Kingdom, Yearbook 1999, p. 77 et seqq.; printed in: EuGRZ 1999, p. 200 et seqq.

35 E.g., judgement of 28.10.1975, Rutili, Case 36/75, ECR 1975, 1219; judgement of 5.3.1980, Pecastaing, Case 98/79, ECR 1980, 691. On this point, see: Manfred A. Dauses, Grundrechte als Elemente einer Verfassungsordnung der Europäischen Union, in: Winfried Böttcher (editor), Europäische Perspektiven, 2002, p. 29.

36 E.g., judgement of 26.6.1997, Familiapress, Case C-368/95, ECR 1997, I-3689, I-3717.

rank higher than the "internal" secondary law, so that they could consequentially be cited as its assessment criterion.[37]

The same also applies for the agreements, such as GATT (1947), which were concluded by the Member States, but the subject-matter of which, according to the substitution principle, meanwhile, comes under the sphere of competence of the Community/Union.[38]

If one combines the *ratio decidendi* of both the case-groups with each other, viz., the higher ranking of the international agreements of the Community/Union vis-à-vis the internal secondary Community/Union law, on the one hand, and the equal hierarchical ranking of the international agreements of the Member States within the scope of application of the Community/Union law with the international agreements of the Community or Union itself, then the conclusion cannot be ruled out that the substantive provisions of the ECHR already exhibit, *de lege lata,* the "trace elements" of a genuine primary Community/Union law.[39]

Where, on the other hand, the level of protection of fundamental rights guarantees in the ECHR in proportion to the fundamental rights in the Community/Union is concerned, the endeavour can be observed as the basic position of the case-law of the ECJ to give the Community/Union law a substance, which fully conforms to the protection requirements of the ECHR as the minimum requirements, i.e., protects the fundamental rights at a level, which should be deemed to be, at least, equivalent to the ECHR.[40]

---

37 Judgement of 30.4.1974, Haegeman, Case 181/73, ECR 1974, 449; judgement of 5.2.1976, Bresciani, Case 87/75, ECR 1976, 129; judgement of 30.11.1977, Cayrol, Case 52/77; ECR 1977, 2261.

38 Judgement of 12.12.1972, International Fruit Company, Case 21-24/72, ECR 1972, 1219, 1226; Judgement of 19.11.1975, Nederlandse Spoorwegen, Case 38/75, ECR 1975, 1439, 1450; judgement of 16.3.1983, Società Italiana per l' Oleodotto Transalpino (SIOT), Case 266/81, ECR 1983, p. 731, 780.

39 Cf. Manfred A. Dauses, Der Schutz der Grundrechte in der Europäischen Gemeinschaft, in: JÖR 1982, p. 1, 16, with references.

40 In this connection, see also judgement of 13.12.1979, Hauer, Case 44/79, ECR 1979, 3727; judgement of 28.10.1975, Rutili, ibid. Explicitly in this connection, see also judgement of 5.3.1980, Pecastaing, ibid., 716: The ECJ had recognised in this judgement that the asserted Community legislation in force fully complies with the requirements of Article 6 ECHR (right to a fair trial), so that it does not require any statements on the logical preliminary question of the relevance of the ECHR in the Community legal order. This judicature is consistent with Article 52(3) 2nd sentence of the European Charter of Fundamental Rights, whereupon the Union law may provide more extensive protection (but not a lower level of protection!) than the ECHR.

3.2.2.4. Excursus: the tense relationship between the Community/Union law and the national law in the area of fundamental rights

At this point, the relationship of the Community/Union law with the national law is discussed in detail in the light of the fundamental rights-related case-law of the European Court of Justice. This relationship is characterised by the structural principles of the autonomy of Community/Union law, its precedence over the national law of any kind and its direct effect ("break-through effect" ["Durchgriffs-wirkung"]) in the national legal order.

a) The European Community/Union has evolved into a legally, sociologically and economically independent legal order. It is "an expression of a special moral consciousness characterised by a European Community of law".[41] The principle of autonomy means that the legal order of the Community/Union flows from its own sources of law, and with increasing concretisation of its fundamental concepts and principles, disengages itself from its basis under the international law, as well as from its historical anchorage in the legal concepts of the Member States. Admittedly, at present, it still appears to be an imperfect partial legal order, which requires the supplementation from the pool of national legal orders with which it is multifariously entwined and interwoven by the commonality of the historical origin. The issue of the European fundamental rights is an example of this statement.

b) Direct effect ("*effet direct*")[42] as the fundamental element of the Community/Union legal order means that all the adequately clear, exact and unconditional communitarian/Union's rules of law – to which also the fundamental rights belong – "can break through" in the sense that they create direct legal relationships, in the national legal sphere, between the governmental authority and the individuals, in fact, under circumstances, even in the mutual relationship of the individuals. The direct effect arises on the basis of the validity claim of Community/Union law itself, without requiring a prior acceptance of the norm in question in the national law by means of a Transformation Act or an enforcement order. So that

41 Ulrich Everling, Sind die Mitgliedstaaten noch Herren der Verträge? Zum Verhältnis von Europäischem Gemeinschaftsrecht und Völkerrecht, in: Festschrift for Hermann Mosler, 1983, p. 173, 177.

42 The concept and scope of the direct effect of the Community law was defined by the ECJ, for the first time, in the leading judgement of 5.2.1963, Van Gend & Loos, Case 26/62, ECR 1963, 1, 24: Community law is more than a classic international law, which is only aimed at the intergovernmental cooperation, and justifies only mutual obligations between the contracting States. The Community is rather, according to the wishes of its founders, an association of European States, having its own autonomous legal order, whose legal subjects are not only the Member States themselves, but the individuals as well.

the Community/Union law concept of "*effet direct [direct effect]*" differs from the international law concept of "*self-executing*" Treaties. The latter qualifies only the basic eligibility of a Treaty provision as regards contents to apply in the national law of the contracting partners, however, says nothing on the actual effect of the provision in the respective national legal sphere.

c) The principle of direct effect is closely linked with the primacy of the Community/Union law, since the inapplicability of inconsistent national law in the lawsuit can be objected to only if the Community/Union law is vested with a higher rank than the national law in the hierarchy of norms. According to the established case-law of the ECJ[43], the priority principle in the Community/Union law enshrines, unlike in international law, not only the obligation of the Member States to harmonise their national law with the higher-ranking Community/Union law, but, in addition, necessitates – in conjunction with the principle of direct effect – that all the national authorities and courts must leave unapplied the inconsistent national law in the cases pending with them, unless it can be interpreted in a way conforming with the Community/Union law.[44] Although this concept does not go so far that the national law, which is contrary to the Community/Union law, loses its validity (priority of validity) *eo ipso*, however, requires that such law should remain out of consideration in case of a conflict (priority of application).

The priority principle is, just as the principle of direct effect, the work of the creative development of the law by the ECJ, which had, for this purpose, stated in the *leading case* of Costa/ENEL "that the law stemming from the Treaty, an independent source of law, could not, because of its special and original nature, be overridden by domestic legal provisions, however framed, without being deprived of its character as Community law and without the legal basis of the Community itself being called into question".[45]

This case-law was strengthened and further developed in a number of subsequent decisions. The ECJ had underlined in them that the hierarchical priority of norms applies to the entire Community law, irrespective of the quality of the respective rule of law. In the opinion of the Community court, the priority principle takes effect even vis-à-vis the national constitutional law, and in fact, even if the concerned national law was passed subsequent to the Community law in question (*lex posterior*).

It may indicate the pleasant status of the implementation of the Community/Union law that the priority principle is recognised today in all the Member States

43 The case-law on the primacy of Community law was introduced with the leading judgement of 15.7.1964, Costa v ENEL, Case 6/64, ECR 1964, 1251, 1268 et seqq.

44 Cf. judgement of 4.2.1988, Murphy, Case 175/86, ECR 1988, 673; see also judgement of 11.7.1989, Ford España, Case 170/88, ECR 1989, 2307.

45 Judgement of 15.7.1964, Costa v ENEL, ibid., 1270.

and is strictly observed by the national courts. Several Member States have included explicit provisions to this effect in their constitutions, which generally declare either the primacy of the international law (or of the international Treaty law) over the national statute law or especially even the primacy of the Community/Union law.

d) Oppositions of fundamental nature against the primacy of the Community/ Union law probably existed only in the area of the fundamental rights. Thus, the Italian *Corte Costituzionale [Constitutional Court]* had although recognised in earlier decisions (1973, 1975 and 1984) the primacy of the Community law over the Italian law, including the constitution, however, raised concerns in case of a violation of the fundamental rights part of the constitution by the acts of the Community institutions.[46]

Even the German Federal Constitutional Court (*Bundesverfassungsgericht,* BVerfG) had expressed reservations in the controversial "*Solange I*" decision of 29.5.1974[47]. The methodical starting point may be seen in the demand that the transfer of sovereign powers to the Community may not lead to an impairment of the protection of fundamental rights guaranteed by the constitutional law. Consequently, sovereign powers could be surrendered to the Community only if a fundamental rights protection, which is consistent with the national standards, is guaranteed in it.

In the meantime, this conflict has been mitigated to a large extent. Since the "*Solange II*" decision of 22.10.1986, the BVerfG now acknowledges that, in the meantime, the ECJ guarantees an effective protection of fundamental rights, which should be considered equivalent to that provided by the German Basic Law, so that

46 Judgment of the *Corte Constituzionale* (Constitutional Court, Italy) of 27.12.1973, in: Giurisprudenza Italiana 1974, I, column 315; Judgment of the *Corte Constituzionale* (Constitutional Court, Italy) of 30.10. 1975, in: Foro Italiano 1975, I, column 2661; Judgment of the *Corte Constituzionale* (Constitutional Court, Italy) of 8.6.1984, in: Foro Italiano 1984, I, column 1251.

47 BVerfGE, vol. 37, p. 271. In this decision, the judicial referral concerning the procedure for the review of the legality pursuant to Article 100(1) Basic Law (GG) was deemed to be admissible, in so far as the clarification was sought on the relationship between the fundamental rights guarantees of the Basic Law and the provisions in the secondary Community law. Although the Community constitutes an autonomous legal order, flowing from an autonomous source of law, however, no sufficient legal certainty for an effective protection of fundamental rights is given, "so long as" the Community legal order has no catalogue of fundamental rights, formulated and adopted by the Parliament, and adequately corresponding to the fundamental rights catalogue of the Basic Law.

the BVerfG no more exercises its jurisdiction on the applicability of secondary Community law in the Federal Republic of Germany:[48]

"So long as the European Communities, in particular, the case law of the Court of Justice of the Communities, generally ensure an effective protection of fundamental rights vis-à-vis the sovereign powers of the Communities which is to be regarded as substantially similar to the protection of fundamental rights required unconditionally by the Basic Law, and in so far as they generally safeguard the essential content of fundamental rights, the Federal Constitutional Court will no longer exercise its jurisdiction to decide on the applicability of secondary Community law cited as the legal basis for any acts of German courts or authorities, and will no longer review such law by the standard of the fundamental rights contained in the Basic Law; corresponding references pursuant to Article 100(1) of the German Basic Law (GG) are therefore inadmissible."

However, the conflict of jurisdiction between the German Supreme Court and the ECJ does not seem to be finally settled yet. Thus, the BVerfG ordained on 12.5.1989 that in case of violations of the communitarian fundamental rights' standards by a Community directive, although the ECJ should grant legal protection in the first place, however, the jurisdiction of the Community court is limited by the protection standards that are deemed indispensable by the Basic Law, the examination of which is subject to the jurisdiction of the BVerfG in the end.[49]

On the other hand, the recent relevant judgement of 12.10.1993 (so-called "Maastricht judgement", concerning the law approving the Union Treaty) evinces an emphasis along the lines of an intensified tendency for the "renationalisation" of the protection of fundamental rights vis-à-vis the sovereign power of the Community/Union. In the said judgement, the BVerfG affirmed its jurisdiction over a general guarantee of an effective protection of fundamental rights within the scope of application of the Basic Law, however, emphasised the intention to exercise its jurisdiction in a "relationship of cooperation" with the ECJ, "in which the European Court of Justice guarantees the protection of fundamental rights in each individual case for the entire area of the European Community; the Federal

48 BVerfG vol. 73, p. 339; on this point, see Meinhard Hilf, Solange II: Wie lange noch Solange?, in: EuGRZ 1987, p. 1; Hubertus Gersdorf, Funktionen der Gemeinschaftsgrundrechte im Lichte des Solange II-Beschlusses des Bundesverfassungsgerichts, in: AÖR 1994, p. 400.

49 So-called "*Wenn nicht*"decision, in: EuGRZ 1989, p. 339 et seqq.; on this point, see, Gert Nicolaysen, Tabakrauch, Gemeinschaftsrecht und Grundgesetz, in: EuR 1989, p. 215; Rupert Scholz, Wie lange bis "Solange III"?, in: NJW 1990, p. 941; cf. also BVerfGE, vol. 75, p. 223, 235; vol. 80, p. 74, 80 et seq. Cf. also Rudolf Streinz, Bundesverfassungsgerichtlicher Grundrechtsschutz und Europäisches Gemeinschaftsrecht, 1989.

Constitutional Court can therefore limit itself to a general guarantee of mandatory fundamental rights standards".[50]

Although until now, the Federal Constitutional Court has not pronounced, in any case, the inapplicability of secondary Community/Union law for the territory of the Federal Republic of Germany due to a violation of the mandatory fundamental rights under the German Basic Law, the principle of "conditional non-application" of the jurisdiction of BVerfG, which is laid down in the "*Solange*" judicature, remains to be a blatant warning to the Community/Union institutions. The German constitutional understanding is, and will probably continue to be, characterised by the maxim that the integration competence of the Basic Law (Article 23 GG) finds its limit in giving up the "identity of the prevailing constitutional order by breaking into its basic framework, that is, into the structure that makes it up.[51]

3.3. Definition and classification of fundamental rights in the light of the case-law of the ECJ

The prevailing European law contains none of the general definitions of the concept of "fundamental rights". Useful indications, which predominantly point at the specific functions of the fundamental rights, arise from the case-law of the ECJ and the legal doctrine. The most important comparisons and delineations will be elaborated in the following.

3.3.1. Fundamental rights and freedoms

A first classification concerns the difference between the fundamental rights and fundamental freedoms within the meaning of the constituent freedoms of the common market/internal market (the free movement of goods, persons, services and capital, Article 26(2) TFEU; ex-Article 14(2) TEC).

Phenotypically, the fundamental freedoms, unlike the fundamental rights, represent the rights, which provide prospects. They open the economic freedom of action for the market participants, and protect them from unjustified restrictions, primarily by the Member States. On the other hand, the guarantee of individual freedom of conduct, with regard to the implementation of the internal market's ob-

50 BVerfGE, vol. 89, p. 155.

51 BVerfGE, vol. 37, p. 271, 279; vol. 73, p. 339, 375 et seq.; vol. 85, p. 191, 203 et seq. See, concerning the state of the dispute: Ulrich Everling, Brauchen wir "Solange III"?, in: EuR 1990, p. 195; Christian Tomuschat, Aller guten Dinge sind III?, in: EuR 1990, p. 340.

jectives, is only a secondary objective, inasmuch as the opening up of the internal market cannot be realised without bestowing subjective rights for the cross-border economic activities.

Another, secondary difference between the fundamental rights and fundamental freedoms is linked to the cross-border or national sphere of influence of the concerned issues: The fundamental freedoms primarily cover the cross-border situations, for which a prohibition of hindrance ("Behinderungsverbot") is applicable. The addressees of this prohibition are primarily the Member States, and not the institutions and bodies of the Community/Union. However, the fundamental rights generally relate, without distinction, to the cross-border and purely internal situations; the addressees of any prohibitions imposed by the fundamental rights are primarily the institutions and bodies of the Community/Union, and the Member States come second within the scope of application of the Union law.[52]

On the other hand, the fundamental rights and fundamental freedoms exhibit diverse points of contact. They overlap, but do not coincide with each other. First of all, it needs to be highlighted that the fundamental freedoms could contain fundamental rights aspects.[53] This is valid, in the first place, for the right to free movement of workers and self-employed persons. It should further be observed that even the restrictions on fundamental freedoms, such as the right to freedom of movement, are, due to the intervention of the authorities of the Member States, subject to fundamental rights-oriented limits. In concrete terms, this means that if a Member State intervenes in a fundamental freedom of the internal market so as to give effect to the mandatory requirements of its national legal order, the measure concerned can only be justified, if it coincides with the fundamental rights under the Community/Union law. In this manner, the fundamental rights limit the Member States' restrictions on market freedoms and ensure the effective application of these freedoms.

3.3.2. Institutional guarantee vs. subjective individual right

The fundamental rights enshrine objective guarantees of institutional rights, on the one hand, and they guarantee subjective individual rights, on the other hand. The

---

52 Udo Ostermann, Entwicklung und gegenwärtiger Stand der europäischen Grundrechte nach der Rechtsprechung des Europäischen Gerichtshofs sowie des Gerichts erster Instanz, ibid., p. 9 et seqq., with references.

53 Alexander Brigola, Das System der EG-Grundfreiheiten: Vom Diskriminierungsverbot zum spezifischen Beschränkungsverbot; the inaugural dissertation was supervised by the author of the present study at the Faculty of Law of the University of Erlangen-Nürnberg, 2004, p. 216 et seq.; cf. also Manfred A. Dauses, Der Schutz der Grundrechte in der Europäischen Gemeinschaft, ibid., p. 2.

function of objective institutional guarantee manifests itself, for instance, by using the example of the freedom of expression and information, which not only aims at the realisation of individual freedoms, but also at the existence and development of the media as the information carriers and communicators.[54] In this latter context belongs the requirement, for example, to maintain and to promote media diversity, i.e., the pluralism of the media landscape. However, the recent case-law of the ECJ is more and more often laying emphasis on the existence of subjective individual rights, and is increasingly placing legal protection of the individuals in the foreground.[55]

3.3.3. Enforceable right vs. programme provisions (soft-law)

Another classification distinguishes between the directly effective, enforceable rights and the non-binding, unenforceable policy clauses and provisions ("*soft law*")[56]. This differentiation often coincides with the differentiation between the subjective individual rights and the objective institutional guarantees. In the existing case-law of the ECJ, the provisions of the "*soft law*" do not play any significant role.

3.3.4. Rights of defence vs. rights to participate

Finally, a differentiation can be made between the rights of defence (negatory rights), on the one hand, and the rights to participate, on the other hand.

Negatory rights guarantee a "*status negativus*". They protect against the sovereign interventions in the freedoms of the individuals by the State, and the authorities attributable to it, or by the Community/Union authorities. As an example of such a right, the freedom of expression and information is again mentioned as an expression of individual intellectual and political freedoms.

---

54 Judgement of 26.6.1997, Familiapress, Case C-368/95, ECR 1997, I-3689, I-3715 et seqq. Cf. also Albert Bleckmann/Stefan Ulrich Pieper, Rechtsquellen, in: Manfred A. Dauses (Hrsg.), Handbuch des EU-Wirtschaftsrechts, B. I., para 124 et seq.

55 In this connection, the ECJ explicitly held, in the judgement of 11.1.2000 (Kreil, Case C-285/98, ECR 2000, I-69, I-104), the right of equal access to employment for men and women guaranteed in the Equal Treatment Directive 76/207 EEC of 9.2.1976 to be an "individual right", to which the plaintiff to the main proceedings, Ms. Tanja Kreil, was entitled.

56 The enforceability of the fundamental rights, as the rights for the protection of individuals, represents the rule in the Community/Union. The "*soft law*" character of the fundamental rights-relevant provisions can be assumed only in exceptional cases, thus, for instance, the prescriptive contents in the social and educational area.

Negatory rights create and, consequently, protect elementary individual spaces of freedom. Thereby, the corresponding rights are not considered as conferred by the State or the society, but as "preceding" the State, and entitled to the individual solely on the basis of his mere existence.

On the other hand, the rights to participate ensure a "*status positivus*" conferred by the State or the society. They make an appearance, primarily as democratic and social civil rights (e.g., voting right, right to education, right to ensure minimum means of subsistence (minimex)).

3.3.5. Equality rights

Equality rights (prohibitions on discrimination) guarantee an equal treatment in similar or comparable situations. As such, they guarantee no absolute, but only a relative standard within the meaning of a right to equal treatment with regard to a given comparable issue. However, equality rights often appear concurrently with the rights of defence or rights to participate. In this combination, they could themselves justify explicit rights to defend or to participate, and could thus bring about the abolition of impositions or grant of preferential treatments.

The Union legal order recognises several specific, as well as general equality rights. Some of them are enshrined in the Union Treaties themselves, others were developed by the case-law of the ECJ.

Specific equality rights unfold their effects in specific, e.g. internal market-related situations. On the other hand, the general prohibitions of discrimination apply to a multitude of diverse situations, thus, for instance, as the comprehensive requirement of equality between women and men (Artikle 3(3) TEU; ex-Article 2 TEC), as directly applicable prohibition of discrimination on grounds of nationality (Article 18 TFEU; ex-Article 12 TEC) or as the general prohibition of discrimination based on sex, racial or ethnic origin, religion or belief, disability, age and sexual orientation (Article 19 TFEU; ex-Article 13 TEC).

However, the written Union law does not recognise a comprehensive definition of the principle of equality. Thus, it was left to the case-law of the ECJ to gradually elaborate, and to give shape to such an overarching general principle. In doing so, it did not rely upon the individual provisions of the Treaties, but inferred a general prohibition of discrimination as an integral part of the general principles of the Community law.[57]

---

57 For the definition and the legal effects of the general principle of equality, see Point 3.6.6. below ("principle of equality")

3.4. Commitment to fundamental rights and entitlement to fundamental rights

In order to be able to restrict the scope *ratione personae* of the Community/ Union law, the sphere of the entities bound by the fundamental rights and the beneficiaries of the fundamental rights is to be defined.

3.4.1. Commitment to fundamental rights

a) An entity committed to the fundamental rights (an addressee of the fundamental rights) is someone who is bound by the fundamental rights. Since the fundamental rights in the Community/Union preferentially serve to protect the citizens from the interventions by the acts of the Community/Union authorities, primarily the institutions and bodies of the Community/Union are bound by these fundamental rights when it comes to legislative process, execution, administration, and dispensation of justice. The obligation encompasses the examination of the validity of the legal acts and any other exercise of sovereign power by the Community/ Union institutions, as well as the interpretation of the entire primary and secondary Community/Union law in the light of the fundamental rights in the Community/ Union.[58]

In this context, the terms “European Community” and “European Union” should be interpreted broadly. They encompass the European Communities or the European Union respectively as the totality of the 3-pillar-structure, as well as their institutions and other bodies, such as the committees or agencies, within the scope of their roles and responsibilities assigned by the European law. Among the latter counts also the European Central Bank, which was established on the basis of the EC Treaty and originally had a legal personality of its own (cf. ex-Article 107(2) TEC). It is now, since the entry into force of the Lisbon Treaty, an institution of the Union (Article 13(1) TEU).

b) But the European fundamental rights not only bind the Community/Union, but under certain conditions even the Member States and the national subdivisions attributable to them.[59] To the latter belong all the public bodies and institutions under State control, whereas it does not make any difference at what level and through which authorities the Member State concerned acts. Consequently, the

---

58 Hans-Werner Rengeling, Grundrechtsschutz in der Europäischen Gemeinschaft, 1993, p. 186 et seqq.; cf. Hans-Werner Rengeling/Peter Szczekalla, Grundrechte in der Europäischen Union – Charta der Grundrechte und allgemeine Rechtsgrundsätze, 2004, p. 137.

59 On this point, see: Dieter Scheuing, Zur Grundrechtsbindung der EU-Mitgliedstaaten, in: EuR 2005, p. 162.

term "Member State" can relate to the central, as well as regional or local levels of action. Likewise, it makes no difference in what function (legislative process, execution, dispensation of justice) the State institution concerned acts. Even an indirect State act, for instance, by legally independent public corporations or institutions, can be attributed to the Member State concerned.

In particular, it is still contentious to what extent the European fundamental rights exactly produce a binding effect vis-à-vis the Member States. Basically, it can be established that the Member States and the institutions and bodies attributable to them are always subject to the communitarian/Union fundamental rights, if they act in the – "real", i.e., not just "potential" – scope of application of Community/Union law, therefore, act determinately from the point of view of European law.[60]

This is especially the case when they implement Community/Union law,[61] e.g., administratively implement Community regulations or decisions[62] or transpose directives in the national law. If, in doing so, they have some options open, they must observe the European fundamental rights when implementing these options. On this note, the judgement of the ECJ in the "Karlsson" case deserves attention: "In addition, it should be remembered that the requirements flowing from the protection of fundamental rights in the Community legal order are also binding on Member States when they implement Community rules".[63]

c) A dogmatic contentious point of discussion concerns the issue, whether, besides the European Community/Union and their Member States, even natural or legal persons, i.e. individuals, could be bound by the fundamental rights. The question at issue is to what extent the European fundamental rights could unfold their effect in private law relationships. This phenomenon is referred to in the German legal terminology as the "third-party effect", in the Community law terminology as the "horizontal effect".

The ECJ has not yet finally answered the issue whether, and to what extent, the European fundamental rights directly apply between private individuals. In principle, such a horizontal effect is contrary to the original meaning of the fundamental rights: These primarily protect the individual from the interventions by the public authorities. However, private law relationships are not characterised just by the relationship of a public authority with an individual, but by the principle of consensus based on the private autonomy. The direct horizontal effect of fundamental

---

60 Albert Bleckmann/Stefan Ulrich Pieper, Rechtsquellen, ibid., B.I., para 149.

61 Cf. Article 51(1) European Charter of Fundamental Rights.

62 Judgement of 25.11.1986, Klensch, Case 201/85, ECR 1986, 3477; judgement of 13.7.1989, Wachauf, Case 5/88, ECR 1989, 2609.

63 Judgement of 13.4.2000, Karlsson, Case C-292/97, ECR 2000, I-2737, para 37.

rights is, therefore, to be looked upon as the exception, and not as the rule, i.e., the fundamental rights do not directly bind the private individuals automatically.[64]

Admittedly, there are specific fields of law, for instance, especially the labour law, in which a direct horizontal effect is, *de lege lata,* already granted to the European fundamental rights. In the first place, the prohibition of difference in salary between men and women for equal work or work of equal value (Article 157 TFEU; ex-Article 141 TEC)[65] can be mentioned. A direct horizontal effect can, moreover, arise from the prohibition of discrimination on grounds of nationality (in particular, Article 18 TFEU; ex-Article 12 TEC).[66]

It must be noted, in addition, that in contrast to the direct horizontal effect, with which the individual can immediately have recourse to the fundamental rights vis-à-vis another person governed by private law, the indirect horizontal effect denotes the influence of fundamental rights on the undefined legal concepts of private law. The ECJ has repeatedly recognised such an influencing effect, thus, for instance, in the judgement in "von Colson-Kamann" case in which, in legal proceedings concerning the principle of equal treatment for men and women as regards access to employment, it held that all the legal norms, which regulate legal relationships between private individuals, should be interpreted in the light of the higher-ranking Community law and, consequently, in the light of the European fundamental rights as well.[67] According to that, the latter are, even if they do not display any direct horizontal effect in the private law relationships, indirectly considerable as interpretive elements in such legal relationships.

3.4.2. Entitlement to fundamental rights

a) All the natural persons, thus all human beings, irrespective of their age and abilities, are to be referred to as the beneficiaries of the fundamental rights. The entitlement to fundamental rights begins with the birth and ends with the death.[68]

64 In this connection, e.g., judgement of 1.10.1987, Vlaamse Reisebureaus, Case 311/85, ECR 1987, 3801, para 30. For the horizontal effect of fundamental rights, see, in general: Albert Bleckmann/Stefan Ulrich Pieper, Rechtsquellen, ibid., B. I., para 130 et seqq.

65 Regarding the predecessor provision Article 119 TEC, for the first time, judgement of 8.4.1976, Defrenne, Case 43/75, ECR 1976, 455.

66 Judgement of 13.12.1984, Haug-Adrion, Case 251/83, ECR 1984, 4277.

67 Judgement of 10.4.1984, Case 14/83, ECR 1984, 1891, para 26, 28. Similarly held by the ECJ in judgement of 6.6.2000, Angonese, Case C-281/98, ECR 2000, I-4139, para 41 et seqq., concerning a publication of a vacancy with factual nationality-related discrimination.

68 Hans D. Jarass, EU-Grundrechte, 2005, p. 43.

Whether even an unborn child, subsequently born alive, can be the beneficiary of the fundamental rights, was not unambiguously decided by the ECJ yet. If, therefore, the issue of the entitlement of the unborn life to the fundamental rights is still open, then, at least, some of the constitutional courts of the Member States have awarded the *nasciturus* (one who is to be born) the protection of the guarantee of human dignity.[69] With regard to the possession of fundamental rights by the children and youth, it is to be observed that it is fundamentally affirmed, unless the relevant European legal basis explicitly presupposes a specific age or a specific ability to reason.

b) However, not only the natural persons could be the beneficiaries of the fundamental rights, even legal persons under private law are entitled to certain fundamental rights. Whether a given fundamental right is applicable also for legal persons, depends on the nature of the specific right.

c) Some fundamental rights, the Union citizens' rights, are explicitly confined to the Union's citizens, i.e., only the citizens of the Member States are entitled to them. Hereby, these are primarily the political freedoms and prerogatives or the fundamental rights, which are closely linked with the fundamental freedoms of the internal market. Other fundamental rights, in turn, are connected to the residence or place of business; they benefit, apart from the Union's citizens, also third-country nationals with residence or place of business in a Member State. Still others favour everybody, irrespective of the nationality or the place of business. The latter are the genuine human rights, which flow directly from the universal human nature.

This differentiation is reminiscent of the German constitutional legal doctrine, which distinguishes between the "rights of the Germans" (the beneficiaries of which can only be "Germans"[70]) and "everyone's rights" (the beneficiary of which can be any person).

d) In principle, the institutions, bodies and agencies of the Union and even of the Member States could not be the beneficiaries of the fundamental rights. It can be otherwise only with regard to the procedural rights or guarantees of legal protection. However, outside this small area of the procedural fundamental rights, a public body can make use of fundamental rights only in exceptional circumstances, viz., if it does not exercise any sovereign power, and is independent of the fundamental rights addressees in pursuing its objectives.[71]

---

69 Hans-Werner Rengeling/Peter Szczekalla, Grundrechte in der Europäischen Union, ibid., p. 197, with references.

70 The German Basic Law uses in its Article 116 the term "German", which has a broader scope than the term "German citizen". It includes "a person who possesses German citizenship or who has been admitted to the territory of the German Reich within the boundaries of 31 December 1937 as a refugee or expellee of German ethnic origin ...".

71 Hans D. Jarass, EU-Grundrechte, ibid., p. 45 et seqq.

3.5. Restrictions on fundamental rights and limits of restrictions on fundamental rights

3.5.1. Preliminary remark

According to the established case-law of the European Court of Justice, the fundamental rights guaranteed in the European Community/Union do not enjoy any unrestricted applicability, but rather "must be viewed in the light of the social function of the property and activities protected thereunder"[72]. Therefore, the exercise of these rights can be subject to restrictions with regard to the objectives serving the general interest of the Community. Such objectives could, e.g., result from the mechanisms of the common market/internal market, the common agricultural policy or from the requirements of any other Community policies, such as the environmental protection, consumer protection or health protection. In order to realise the predominant economic objectives of the Community/Union, efficient regulations are needed, the implementation of which is not always possible without interventions in the rights of individuals.

Since, consequently, the use of fundamental rights, which is not subjugated to any regulations, would lead to conflicts with the interests of the public in general and also with the fundamental and human rights of other rights-holders,[73] it is necessary to develop the exact content and scope of the fundamental and human rights. Thereby, the possibilities of imposing restrictions on the use of these rights must be discussed in detail.

In order to assess whether a fundamental right was violated, it is to be clarified, first of all, whether the scope of protection of the fundamental right concerned was affected by a measure, which could qualify as an intervention, and thereafter, whether the intervention can be justified. The scope of protection pertains to the object of impairment of fundamental rights, and describes the potential scope of a specific fundamental right.[74] Interventions are referred to as measures, which

---

72 Judgement of 14.5.1974, Nold, Case 4/73, ECR 1974, 491, 507; judgement of 13.12.1979, Hauer, Case 44/79, ECR 1979, 3727, 3749; judgement of 11.7.1989, Schräder, Case 256/87, ECR 1989, 2237, 2268; judgement of 13.7.1989, Wachauf. Case 5/88, ECR 1989, 2609, 2639; judgement of 24.8.1998, Metronome Musik, Case C-200/96, ECR 1998, I-1953, I-1978. On this point, see: Urs Schildknecht, Grundrechtsschranken in der Europäischen Gemeinschaft, 2000, p. 49.

73 Cf. Detlef Merten/Hans-Jürgen Papier, Handbuch der Grundrechte, 2004, p. 300.

74 In this regard, the ECJ has been accused on various occasions that it omits a clear determination of the scope of protection in question and, instead, instantly passes over to the review of any grounds of justification for the intervention in the right concerned: Rudolf Streinz, Bundesverfassungsgerichtlicher Grundrechtsschutz und Europäisches

constitute an impairment of the fundamental rights, and are characterised, in the broadest sense, by an onerous or detrimental effect.

Limits are restrictions on fundamental rights. They are permissible, if they are justified. Above all, the "objectives of general interest recognised by the Union"[75] and the "need to protect the rights and freedoms of others"[76] have been highlighted as the grounds of justification in the case-law of the ECJ. The so-called "limits of restrictions", in which the principle of proportionality and the guarantee of the substance (essential content) have key priority, result in that the restrictions on fundamental rights, on their part, are again subject to limitations, which make sure that the interventions in the Community fundamental rights are not permissible without limits. The clearer the mentioned elements are stipulated in the Community law and counterbalanced by the case-law, the more exists legal certainty with regard to the spaces of freedom accorded to the citizen.

In the following, the restrictions and the limits of restrictions on the fundamental rights in the Community/Union will be discussed in detail.

3.5.2. Restrictions on fundamental rights

As already mentioned above, the exercise of the communitarian/Union fundamental rights is primarily subject to two immanent restrictions: Restrictions for reasons of protecting the general public interest and restrictions with regard to the rights and freedoms of others.

The fundamental rights restrictions with regard to "objectives serving the general interest of the Community" need a special comment. In this regard, the ECJ has developed three criteria of justification:

- the intervention in the fundamental right concerned must pursue objectives of the general interest of the Community;
- the intervention must be proportional with regard to these objectives;
- the substance of the protected rights must remain untouched.[77]

These criteria could not be applied schematically, but should be evaluated in their specific and individual context. Finally, a balance between the requirements of

---

Gemeinschaftsrecht, 1989, p. 403; Albert Bleckmann, Die Rechtsquellen des Europäischen Gemeinschaftsrechts, in: NVwZ 1993, p. 824, 827.

75 Judgement of 14.5.1974, Nold, ibid.; judgement of 13.7.1989, Wachauf, ibid.

76 Judgement of 26.6.1997, Familiapress, Case C-368/95, ECR 1997, I-3689, I-3717.

77 Judgement of 13.12.1979, Hauer, ibid.; judgement of 13.7.1989, Wachauf, ibid.; judgement of 17.7.1997, SAM Schifffahrt, Case C-248/95 and C-249/95, ECR 1997, I-4475, para 72.

the fundamental right concerned and the reasons of public interest, which could justify the intervention in this right, must be established.[78]

In this respect, the ECJ has been accused that it devaluates the fundamental rights restrictions with regard to "objectives serving the general interest of the Community" to an indeterminate, largely meaningless empty phrase, which could cover an extremely wide range of objectives.[79] Actually, this phrase is construed in a very broad sense, so that it becomes operable only after mentioning a specific objective in the public interest. But this step is often omitted; the ECJ rather considers the interventions in the scope of protection of the fundamental rights to be justified, if any Community objective is pursued therewith. As a result, it often outlines the asserted objective in the public interest only summarily (implementation of internal market; stabilisation of agricultural markets etc.), without specifying it in detail, and analysing it for its value.[80] Thus, the Community/Union legislator is granted a very wide discretion to implement measures, which could bring about interventions in the fundamental rights.

3.5.3. Limits of restrictions on fundamental rights

In order to limit the scope of discretion, which is connected to the restrictions in the general public interest, the principle of proportionality and the guarantee of the substance (essential content) are mentioned as the general limits of restrictions ("Schranken-Schranken"). They serve as correctives to protect from excessive interventions in the fundamental rights.

The starting point of the doctrine of the limits of restrictions is the ascertainment that even the restrictive provisions could not be stipulated arbitrarily, but are, on their part, subject to specific conditions, which restrict them in turn. This graduated system is the consequence of the constitutional principle of the highest possible degree of efficiency of the fundamental rights[81].

---

78 In the German Constitutional theory, this balance is termed as "practical concordance".

79 Cf. Dieter Feger, Die Normsetzung auf dem Gebiet der Grundrechte in den Europäischen Gemeinschaften – Der Europäische Gerichtshof (EuGH) als Rechtsetzungsorgan, in: DÖV 1987, p. 322, 330.

80 Judgement of 17.7.1997, SAM Schifffahrt, ibid.

81 Gunter M. Hoffmann, Grundrechte in Europa – braucht Europa einen Grundrechtskatalog?, 1995, p. 57; cf. also Albert Bleckmann, Staatsrecht II – Die Grundrechte, 3rd edition 1989, p. 301 et seqq.

3.5.3.1. Limits of restrictions on proportionality

The key principle of proportionality enables the mitigation of hardships and the balancing of conflicting interests. A comprehensive definition of this principle can be found in the judgement in the "Schräder" case:[82]

"(...) The principle of proportionality is recognised by the established case-law of the Court as being part of the general principles of the Community law. By virtue of that principle, measures imposing financial charges on economic operators are lawful provided that they are appropriate and necessary for attaining the objectives legitimately pursued by the rules in question. However, when there is a choice between several appropriate measures, the least onerous measure must be used and the charges imposed must not be disproportionate to the aims pursued. (...)"

An analysis of this *leading case* evinces the following sub-elements of the principle of proportionality:

- the suitability, i.e., the measure intervening in the fundamental right must be appropriate for the realisation of the objectives which are in the general public interest;
- the necessity, i.e., from among several appropriate measures, that measure must be selected, which is the least onerous for the parties involved: A less drastic means must not be given with which the pursued objective can be achieved just as well;
- the appropriateness (prohibition of disproportionate measures), i.e., the detriments caused by the intervention must be in an appropriate proportion to the strived objective, or the measure must not represent any unbearable intervention with regard to the pursued objective. At the same time, the Community's interest in the implementation of the measure at issue must be weighed against the individual interest in the protection from charges; advantages and disadvantages of the measure must be in a balanced proportion to each other.[83]

Consequently, the significant function of the principle of proportionality is to restrict the Community/Union legislator in its scope of discretion with regard to the public interest provisos,[84] on the one hand, and, on the other hand, to deliver the

---

82 Judgement of 11.7.1989, Case 265/87, ECR 1989, 2237, 2269. On this point, see also Point 3.6.7. below ("principle of proportionality").

83 Concerning the prohibition of disproportionate measures, see also: judgement of 10.1.1992, Kühn, Case C-177/90, ECR 1992, I-35; judgement of 17.7.1997, Affish, Case C-183/95, ECR 1997, I-4315.

84 Detlef Merten/Hans-Jürgen Papier, Handbuch der Grundrechte, ibid., p. 896.

criteria, as a general restrictive regulation, for maintaining the balance, which is requisite for the realisation of the fundamental rights, between the individual and the general public interests. In this context, the judicial review – often perceived as too lax by the critics – represents a practical problem. Actually, it should not be overlooked that the Court has, in its case-law when weighing the values and interests in the area of the protection of fundamental rights, left the Community/Union institutions with a very wide scope of discretion.[85] This is seen especially in complex economic matters in which the Court has affirmed a violation of the fundamental rights only with extreme hesitation in most cases, viz., when the measure at issue is "manifestly inappropriate",[86] "manifestly erroneous"[87] or "manifestly disproportionate"[88]. It is to be observed, moreover, that the scope of judicial review of the normative provisions is clearly lesser than that of the provisions on case-by-case basis, which the ECJ subjects to a closer examination in general.

3.5.3.2. Limits of restrictions on the guarantee of the substance (essential content)

In addition to the key principle of proportionality, the guarantee of the substance can be determined as the second general limit of restrictions. According to the abstract, general point of view prevailing in the literature, the substance of a fundamental right is guaranteed, if generally an inviolable core area remains, i.e., the relevant fundamental right remains guaranteed as an institution, even if, in a specific individual case, it is deprived of its substance (essential content). On the other hand, according to the specific, individual point of view, the focus should be on whether a core-guarantee of fundamental rights is retained in each individual case. The statements of the ECJ do not show any clear preference for either of these theories so far, however, in a few judgements, indications can be found in favour of an individual definition of the inviolable core content of the respectively relevant Community fundamental right.[89]

---

85 Cf. Georg Berrisch, Zum "Bananen"-Urteil des EuGH of 5.10.1994 – Case C-280/93, Germany v Council of the European Union, EuR 1994, p. 461, 466.

86 Judgement of 11.7.1989, Schräder, ibid.

87 Judgement of 5.10.1994, Germany v Council, Case C-280/93, ECR 1994, I-4973, I-5068 et seq.

88 Judgement of 13.12.1994, Winzersekt, Case C-306/93, ECR 1994, I-5555, I-5583; judgement of 6.12.2001, Area Cova, Case T-196/99, EuGE 2001, II-3597, II-3643.

89 Cf. judgement of 13.7.1989, Wachauf, Case 5/88, ECR 1989, 2609, 2639 et seq., concerning an expropriation without compensation. On this point, see: Ingolf Pernice, Gemeinschaftsverfassung und Grundrechtsschutz – Grundlagen, Bestand, Perspektiven, in: NJW 1990, p. 2409, 2416; Theodor Schilling, Bestand und allgemeine Lehren der bürgerschützenden allgemeinen Rechtsgrundsätze des Gemeinschaftsrechts, in: EuGRZ 2000, p. 3, 12.

In this context, it is to be pointed out that the casuistry of the ECJ is inconsistent for the interaction of the principle of proportionality and the guarantee of the substance (essential content). Although the Court considers the guarantee of the substance predominantly as its own limit on restrictions, besides the principle of proportionality,[90] however, in several other judgements, it has treated it as an integral part of the review of the proportionality and, in this respect, it has equated it with the examination of the appropriateness (prohibition of disproportionate measures), without awarding it an independent semantic content.[91]

3.6. Individual fundamental rights recognised by the case-law of the ECJ

In the following, the most important fundamental rights in Community/Union law, developed by the judicature of the European Court of Justice, including the basic principles of the rule of law and the fundamental rights-related general principles of administrative law, will be discussed. In this connection, especially the following rights will be analysed: a) human dignity; b) right to property; c) freedom to pursue economic activities; d) freedom of expression and religion; e) respect for private and family life; f) principle of equal treatment; g) principle of proportionality; h) fundamental procedural rights.

3.6.1. Human dignity

The human dignity occupies the highest position in the hierarchy of the fundamental rights developed by the case-law of the ECJ. It represents the highest individual legal interest, which should be respected and protected. Although the ECJ does not explicitly refer to the concept of human dignity, however, rudimentarily makes to understand, at least in two incidents, that its decision is essentially based upon the commitment to a highest fundamental humanistic value, which exaggerates all other values, influences them and pierces them. The judgements in this regard were based on a discrimination on grounds of sex change,[92] on the one hand, and

90 Rudolf Streinz, Bundesverfassungsgerichtlicher Grundrechtsschutz und Europäisches Gemeinschaftsrecht, 1989, p. 422; Urs Schildknecht, Grundrechtsschranken in der Europäischen Gemeinschaft, ibid., p. 92 et seqq.

91 Judgement of 5.10.1994, Germany v Council, Case C-280/93, ibid.

92 Judgement of 30.4.1996, P v S and Cornwall County Council, Case C-13/94, ECR 1996, I-2143, I-2165.

a procedure for the annulment of a directive for the legal protection of biotechnological inventions, on the other hand[93].

3.6.2. *Right to property*

Because of the predominant economic nature of the Community/Union, a not insignificant portion of the decided fundamental rights cases relate to the protection of fundamental economic and social rights. First among these is the right to property.

The right to property possesses a dual character: On the one hand, it is an integral part of the objective legal order and value system of the Community/Union, inasmuch as the private property is permitted and protected as such, i.e., can be acquired, used and transferred. Within this meaning, Article 345 TFEU (ex-Article 295 TEC) guarantees: "The Treaties shall in no way prejudice the rules in Member States governing the system of property ownership." On the other hand, the ownership is a subjective individual right, which combines the aspects of a right of defence and a right to participate. The jurisprudence of the ECJ refers, almost without exception, to this latter aspect.

Three earlier judgements of the ECJ are taken as examples, which were already pointed out above in connection with the doctrine of the sources of law in the area of the fundamental rights, viz., the judgements in the cases of Internationale Handelsgesellschaft,[94] Nold[95] and Hauer.[96] Hereof, the judgement in the Hauer case is especially illuminative: In the said case, the ECJ had distinguished between the expropriation, i.e., the deprivation of the property within the meaning of a deprivation of the substance of ownership, and mere regulations of its use. The expropriations could only be justified by compelling public interest requirements, whereas mere usage restrictions only require reasonable considerations of the public interest for their justification. Moreover, the Hauer case deserves attention also because, in this case, the ECJ undertook an in-depth analysis of the specific sources of law, which guarantee the right to property, viz., analysis of

---

93 Judgement of 9.10.2001, Netherlands v Parliament and Council, Case C-377/98, ECR 2001, I-7079, I-7168.

94 Judgement of 17.12.1970, Case 11/70, ibid.

95 Judgement of 14.5.1974, Case 4/73, ibid.

96 Judgement of 13.12.1979, Case 44/79, ibid. On this point, see: Ingolf Pernice, Grundrechtsgehalte im europäischen Gemeinschaftsrecht – Ein Beitrag zum gemeinschaftsimmanenten Grundrechtsschutz durch den Europäischen Gerichtshof, 1979, p. 135; Christine von Milczewski, Der grundrechtliche Schutz des Eigentums im Europäischen Gemeinschaftsrecht, 1994, p. 60; Jürgen Michael Thiel, Europa 1992: Grundrechtlicher Eigentumsschutz im EG-Recht, in: JuS 1991, p. 274.

Article 1 of the Additional Protocol to the European Convention on Human Rights and the relevant provisions in the constitutions of the Member States.[97]

In the light of the considerations of the judgment in the Hauer case, the area of conflict between the Community's protection of fundamental rights and the economic objectives of the Community is highlighted especially well. That judgement indicates that the protection of property ownership should be evaluated, above all, against the background of the commitment to the "principle of an open market economy with free competition", contained in Article 4 TEC (now: Article 119 TFEU), because the functioning of the market economy mechanisms is not conceivable without the existence of private ownership of the means of production. Therefore, the protection of individual proprietary positions vis-à-vis the sovereign acts of the Community earns a special interest with regard to the realisation of the economic objectives of the Community. More specifically, the ECJ states in the grounds of the judgement in the Hauer case:

- With regard to the communitarian prohibition on the new planting of vines at issue, one cannot speak of a deprivation of the property because the owner still had the power to dispose of the property or to put it to other uses; she could sell it, use it, mortgage it, destroy it or use it in any other non-prohibited manner. Rather the impairment of the fundamental right at issue is a mere control of the use of property.
- In order to assess the legality of this control, the ECJ refers to the constitutional provisions and the constitutional practice of individual Member States. It observes that all the wine producing Member States have provisions at the national level, which are similar to the Community provision at issue. But if a national legislator is empowered to control the use of private property in accordance with the general public interest, the Community should be entitled to the same as well. Such a restriction may be permitted, if it is in the interest of the general welfare of the Community and fits in its structure and objectives.
- In order to establish whether the mentioned conditions exist in the present case, the Court now examines whether the prohibition on new planting of vines, which was decided for reasons of structural policy in the context of the common organisation of the market for wine, in fact "correspond to objectives of general interest pursued by the Community". Within this context, it refers to the principle of proportionality and the guarantee of the substance (essential content) for the protection from intervention: The prohibition on new planting of vines may "with regard to the aim pursued, ... not constitute a disproportionate and intolerable interference with the rights of the owner, such as to impinge upon the very substance of the right to property".[98]

In addition, it is pointed out that according to recent decisions of the ECJ, market shares as such do not fall under the right to property.[99] However, the production

97 Judgement of 13.12.1979, Case 44/79, ibid., 3745.
98 Judgement of 13.12.1979, Hauer, Case 44/79, ibid., 3747.
99 Judgement of 23.10.1991, von Deetzen, Case C-44/89, ECR 1991, I-5119, I-5156.

quota, which a producer has acquired as the fruit of his labour and his investments, is entitled to the protection of property ownership; as a result, it cannot be taken from the owner of such a quota without compensation.[100]

3.6.3. Freedom to pursue economic activities

The freedom to pursue economic activities has found its way into the case-law of the ECJ under various names, thus, for instance, as "freedom of occupation, freedom to pursue trade or professional activities"[101] or as the right of "freedom to exercise a profession".[102] These freedoms and rights compete, in most cases of application, with the right to property. In such cases, the Court tends to cite the same or similar criteria for the justification of interventions in the scope of protection of both the categories of the fundamental rights.

Thus, the ECJ had pronounced in the *leading case* Hauer with great clarity that if the prohibition on new planting of vines could affect the free pursuit of the occupation of wine-growing, that limitation is no more than the consequence of the restriction upon the exercise of the right to property, so that the two restrictions merge. Thus, the restriction upon the free pursuit of the occupation of wine growing, assuming that it exists, is justified by the same reasons which justify the restriction placed upon the use of property.[103] In other cases, the Court simply restricted itself to examine together the asserted violations of the right to property and the freedom to pursue economic activities, which referred to the same factual situation.

Irrespective of the presented methodical approach, the Court inclines to differentiate, as regards the criteria of justification for the interventions in the freedom to choose an occupation (much like in the case-law of the German Constitutional Court), between the freedom of access to a profession[104] and the freedom to exercise a profession[105]. In both the cases, the interventions are subject to the principle of proportionality, however, more stringent requirements are imposed on the implementation of this leading principle, if it concerns the access to a profes-

100 Judgement of 13.7.1989, Wachauf, Case 5/88, ibid.
101 Judgement of 14.5.1974, Nold, Case 4/73, ibid.,507.
102 Judgement of 13.12.1979, Hauer, Case 44/79, ibid., 3750.
103 Judgement of 13.12.1979, Hauer, Case 44/79, ibid.
104 Judgement of 15.10.1987, Unectef v Heylens, Case 222/86, ECR 1987, 4097, 4117.
105 Judgement of 11.7.1989, Schräder, Case 265/87, ECR 1989, 2237, 2268.

sion – the restrictions on which affect especially severely –, than if it's a matter of mere modalities of the exercise of the profession.[106]

In this connection, it is pointed out that the judicature of the ECJ even shows the indications of a fundamental rights-worthy general freedom of action.[107] In the literature, it is still not finally clarified whether this is to be understood as an expansion of the various forms of freedom to pursue economic activities, therefore, as an economically justified auxiliary freedom, or rather as an independent first principle, which intervenes as a subsidiary right, if no specific economic provision is relevant.[108]

3.6.4. Freedom of expression and religion

The freedom of expression, including the freedom to hold opinions and the freedom to receive and impart information and ideas, is stipulated in detail in Article 10 of the European Convention on Human Rights. It is primarily an intellectual right, which, however, also comprises commercial aspects, thus the "*right of commercial speech*". Against this background, it is not surprising that the European Court of Justice had, in a multitude of judgements which concerned the right to the freedom of expression and information under the Community law, explicitly reverted to the aforementioned provisions of the ECHR and the relevant judgements of the European Court of Human Rights as the sources of the knowledge of law.[109]

With regard to the legal-system's classification, the freedom of expression and information is primarily developed as a subjective individual right, but also manifests itself as an objective institutional guarantee, for it cannot unfold its beneficial effect without the functioning mechanisms to guarantee effective and independent media in a democratic, pluralistic media society. From this perspective, the ECJ had, at the same time, inferred from the individual fundamental right of expression and information the objective obligation of the Member States to ensure the protection of pluralism in the media.[110]

---

106 Cf. Udo Ostermann, Entwicklung und gegenwärtiger Stand der europäischen Grundrechte nach der Rechtsprechung des Europäischen Gerichtshofs sowie des Gerichts erster Instanz, ibid., p. 186, with references from the case-law and the literature.

107 Judgement of 21.5.1987, Rau, Case 133-136/85, ECR 1987, 2289, 2339.

108 With regard to the last point: Walter Pauly, Strukturfragen des unionsrechtlichen Grundrechtsschutzes, in: EuR 1998, p. 242, 254; Theodor Schilling, ibid., p. 14.

109 References by Udo Ostermann, ibid., p. 169.

110 Judgement of 26.6.1997, Familiapress, Case C-368/95, ECR 1997, I-3689, I-3715 et seqq.; cf. also judgement of 25.7.1991, Gouda, Case C-288/89, ECR 1991, I-4007,

The freedom of conscience and religion (guaranteed in Article 9 ECHR) has in common with the freedom of expression and information that it embodies a prototypical intellectual fundamental right. Due to the key economic focus of the Community, it was brought up before the ECJ only in a few legal proceedings, for instance, in an earlier EC-officials' case. In this case, the Court of Justice was called upon to decide on the action brought by a job applicant, who refused to participate in a competition (selection process) on a religious holiday, which was not a legal holiday in Belgium. The ECJ underlined the high value of the freedom of conscience and religion in the Community legal order, however, dismissed the prayer for relief on the ground that the candidate had failed to inform the appointing authority of her religious beliefs in due time.[111]

3.6.5. Respect for private and family life

According to the emphasis of the field of activity of the Community, the protection of private and family life has received little exposure in the case-law of the ECJ. Apart from one case, which concerned the clandestine performance of an AIDS-test and, at the same time, the violation of the right to the privacy of health status,[112] the precedents are linked, almost without exception, to the exercise of market freedoms or the rules of competition. This is explained not least by that the Court of Justice had interpreted the concept of "private life" in such a broad manner that occupational activities are basically not excluded from it.[113]

Thus, for instance, the fundamental right to respect for family life can be affected by the difficulties in the area of the right to subsequent immigration of the family members of the migrant workers. Such an impermissible difficulty can exist, for example, in that the subsequent immigration of the family is contingent on the condition that the family has an accommodation in the host country, which meets the normal requirements of the host country.[114]

I-4043; Jürgen Kühling, Grundrechtskontrolle durch den EuGH: Kommunikationsfreiheit und Pluralismussicherung im Gemeinschaftsrecht, in: EuGRZ 1997, p. 296.

111 Judgement of 27.10.1976, Prais, Case 130/75, ECR 1976, 1589, 1598 et seq. On this point, see: Winfried Bausback, Religions- und Weltanschauungsfreiheit als Gemeinschaftsgrundrecht, in: EuR 2000, p. 261.

112 Judgement of 5.10.1994, X v Commission, Case C-404/92, ECR 1994, I-4737, I-4789.

113 Judgement of 20.5.2003, Österreichischer Rundfunk, Case C-465/00, C-138/01 and C-139/01, ECR 2003, I-4989, I-5043.

114 Judgement of 18.5.1989, Commission v Germany, Case 249/86, ECR 1989, 1263, 1290. In this judgement, the ECJ interpreted the relevant (annulled in the meantime) secondary law provisions on the right to subsequent immigration of the family re-

The right to confidentiality of the written communications between a lawyer and his client, which is known as "*legal privilege*" in the legal circles of the Common Law, and is considered as a significant specificity of the leading principle of the "*due process*", was recognised as a Community fundamental right by the ECJ in connection with the investigative powers of the Commission in the European competition law, provided the confidant is an independent lawyer, i.e., not appointed by the client. Consequently, the Commission was prohibited to inspect the confidential documents and to use them for the investigative procedure.[115]

Along a similar line was the ECJ judgement in the "Hoechst" case, concerning the investigative powers of the Commission as the European competition regulatory authority. The Court of Justice made a methodologically unobjectionable and result-oriented Solomonic determination by awarding, based on a comparative legal analysis of the legal orders of the Member States (twelve at that time), the protection of fundamental right to the inviolability of the private residence, not, however, of the business premises. Only the former is, as an integral part of the private life, fundamentally protected against the administrative searches, whereas interventions in the integrity of the business premises are only subject to certain procedural guarantees and the overriding principle of proportionality.[116]

3.6.6. Principle of equality

In the Community legal order, the general principle of equality plays a prominent role, which, as an overarching principle of law, comprises several prohibitions on discrimination. As already indicated above (Point 3.3.5), although the written Community law enshrines several more or less specific requirements of

---

strictively within the meaning that the requirement, to live in appropriate housing conditions, although must be asserted when the first resident permit is issued for the members of the family, however, not when it is extended.

115 Judgement of 18.5.1982, AM&S, Case 155/79, ECR 1982, 1575, 1610 et seq. From the methodology point of view, it may astonish that in this judgement, the Court of Justice arrived at an assumption of a (procedural) Community fundamental right. Actually, such a corresponding right cannot be found in the ECHR. In addition, "constitutional traditions common to the Member States" can hardly be spoken of if only two States with Common Law – Tradition (United Kingdom and Ireland) guarantee a "*legal privilege*" in their national legal orders. On this point, see, Claudia Seitz, Der Vertraulichkeitsschutz der Anwaltskorrespondenz im europäischen Wettbewerbsverfahren – zu Umfang und Ausgestaltung des Anwaltsgeheimnisses nach der neueren europäischen Rechtsprechung, in: EuZW 2008, p. 204.

116 Judgement of 21.9.1989, Hoechst, Case 46/87 and 227/88, ECR 1989, 2859, 2924. See also Point 3.2.2.2. above ("Member States' constitutional traditions").

equal treatment, however, recognises – just as the European Convention on Human Rights – no abstract general principle of equality. Such a principle had rather to be defined by the ECJ only.

Within the scope of this praetorian process, remarkably, the ECJ did not start with a comparative overall perspective of individual provisions of the Treaties, rather recognised the principle of equality as an integral part of the general principles of the Community law, which belongs to the foundations of this law and has found specific expressions in the individual areas. The Court of Justice specified the "equality of treatment in the matter of economic rules"[117] and the "principle of equal distribution of public burdens"[118] as expressions of prohibitions on discrimination over and above those specifically contained in the Community Treaties. In its most general definition, the principle of equality states that a difference in treatment is permissible only "if [it] corresponds to a difference in the situations".[119] *Vice versa*, "comparable situations should not be treated differently, unless the different treatment is objectively justified".[120] It is obvious that the cited wording is significant only if both the comparable situations lie in the scope of application of the Community law.

Violations of the principle of equality are, if the discrimination brings about an unjustified burden, eliminated by that the discriminating measure is declared by the judgement – depending upon the type of procedure – to be "void", "invalid" or "inapplicable". However, under the circumstance that the discrimination exists in the denial of a privilege, the interest of the party concerned in its own betterment cannot be satisfied by annulling the discriminating provision because, thus, all the legitimate beneficiaries would be deprived of the advantage. On the other hand, however, the power of the judiciary to grant the benefit that is sought seems doubtful because, as a rule, several possibilities exist to restore equality of treatment. The Court has solved the dilemma in the manner that it has declared the discriminating provision incompatible only with the principle of equality, and has asked the competent political institutions to restore equality of treatment, at their options, in their own judgement of the relevant economic and political viewpoints.[121]

---

117 Judgement of 21.6.1958, Groupement des Hauts Fourneaux et Aciéries belges, Case 8/57, ECR 1958, 233.

118 Judgement of 13.7.1961, Meroni, Case 14, 16, 17, 20, 24, 26, 27/60, and 1/61, ECR 1961, 347, 364 et seq.

119 Judgement of 21.6.1958, Groupement des Hauts Fourneaux et Aciéries belges, ibid.

120 Judgement of 19.10.1977, "Quellmehl", Case 117/76 and 16/77, ECR 1977, 1753, 1770 et seq.; Judgement of 19.10.1977, "Maisgritz", Case 124/76 and 20/77, ECR 1977, 1795, 1812 et seq.

121 Ibidem. The parallel to the practice of the German Federal Constitutional Court is unmistakable, which, in cases in which "several options are available" to the legislator "to create the equality required by the Constitution", contents itself with the mere

3.6.7. Principle of proportionality

The principle of proportionality as a means for constitutionally required limitations of sovereign power is a key integral part of every national legal order. In the European law, it is already rooted in the early case-law of the ECJ.[122] Thereby, first of all, it was assigned an alternative function for safeguarding the individuals' interests, which were worthy of protection as fundamental rights; it was understood in the broadest sense as an expression of the overarching principle of justice.

Within this meaning, the ECJ stated in the judgement in the Klöckner and Hoesch cases, that "the aims pursued must be attained under the most favourable conditions and with the smallest possible sacrifices by the undertakings affected".[123] In a later case, it held that the Community institutions must ensure, in the exercise of their powers, "that the amounts which commercial operators are charged are no greater than is required to achieve the aim which the authorities are to accomplish."[124]

If, initially, the principle of proportionality simply formed a corrective against the excessive effects of overly rigid law, it gradually developed into an inherent leading communitarian principle with substance of fundamental rights or, at least, substance similar to fundamental rights. The following comprehensive definition in the judgement in the Schräder case shows this: "Measures imposing financial charges on economic operators are lawful provided that they are appropriate and necessary for attaining the objectives legitimately pursued by the rules in question. However, when there is a choice between several appropriate measures, the least onerous measures must be used and the charges imposed must not be disproportionate to the aims pursued."[125]

If one observes the cited definition, it can be recognised easily that it has a wider scope than the scope of application of the Treaty provision under Article 5(4) TEU (ex-Article 5(3) TEC), which restricts the exercise of the Union's competences

---

determination of the unconstitutionality and refrains from a declaration of annulment (e.g., BVerfGE vol. 22, p. 361; vol. 23, p. 10; vol.25, p. 252).

122 The principle of proportionality was mentioned, for the first time, in the judgement "Fedechar": judgement of 29.11.1956, Fédération Charbonnière de Belgique v High Authority, Case 8/55, ECR 1955/56, 297, 311.

123 Judgement of 13.7.1962, Klöckner und Hoesch, Cases 17/61 and 20/61, ECR 1962, 653, 686.

124 Judgement of 24.10.1973, Balkan, Case 5/73, ECR 1973, 1091, 1112; judgement of 24.10.1973, Schlüter, Case 9/73, ECR 1973, 1135, 1155.

125 Judgement of 11.7.1989, Schräder, Case 265/87, ECR 1989, 2237, 2269. On this point, see also Point 3.5.3.1. above ("limits of restrictions on proportionality").

to what is necessary for the achievement of the objectives of the Treaties.[126] This competence standard strictly limits the proportionality test to the first and second test levels (suitability and necessity of the measure), excluding the third level (appropriateness of the measure, i.e., prohibition of disproportionate measures).

The preceding statements must have made it clear that the principle of proportionality is assigned a subjective protective function not only – as depicted above (Point 3.5.3.1.) – as a limit of restrictions in case of interventions in the scope of protection of the fundamental rights, but also in its expression as an independent general principle of law having the significance of a fundamental right[127]; it generally tempers the interventions in the individual rights.[128]

3.6.8. Basic procedural rights

In the case-law of the ECJ, the fundamental rights-related general principles of the rule of law and of procedural law also have a prominent significance ("*due process*");[129] the following principles rank first:

---

126 Article 5(4) TEU says *verbatim*: "Under the principle of proportionality, the content and form of Union action shall not exceed what is necessary to achieve the objectives of the Treaties".

127 Cf. Udo Ostermann, Entwicklung und gegenwärtiger Stand der europäischen Grundrechte nach der Rechtsprechung des Europäischen Gerichtshofs sowie das Gerichts erster Instanz, ibid., p. 198 et seq., with reference, among others, to Ingolf Pernice/ Franz Mayer, in: Eberhard Grabitz/Meinhard Hilf, Das Recht der Europäischen Union, Kommentar, nach Art. 6 EUV, para 306. Cf. also Urs Schildknecht, Grundrechtsschranken in der Europäischen Gemeinschaft, 2000, p. 49.

128 In connection with the review of proportionality, the ECJ has been accused, time and again, that it only pays lip service to the principle of proportionality, but lacks the courage for cassation. Moreover, weighing the private interests of the fundamental rights-holders against the Community's interests leads to a systematic bias in favour of the Community and to the detriment of the individuals. Above all, it is criticised that the ECJ does not undertake any stringent stipulation of the scope of protection of the fundamental rights, and any determination and assessment of the protected individual interests, but instead, quite frequently goes over directly to the issue whether the challenged measure is supported by the Community's interests, and therewith, serves the general public interest. See also, Manfred A. Dauses, Grundrechte als Elemente einer Verfassungsordnung der Europäischen Union, in: Winfried Böttcher, Europäische Perspektiven, 2002, p. 29, 38. Cf. Uwe Kischel, Die Kontrolle der Verhältnismäßigkeit durch den Europäischen Gerichtshof, in: EuR 2000, p. 380; Martin Nettesheim, Grundrechtliche Prüfdichte durch den EuGH, in: EuZW 1995, p. 106.

129 On these issues, see, in general: Jürgen Schwarze, Europäisches Verwaltungsrecht – Entstehung und Entwicklung im Rahmen der Europäischen Gemeinschaft, 1988.

a) legal certainty; b) protection of legitimate expectations; c) right to a hearing; d) right against self-incrimination; e) the ne bis in idem principle. The principle of confidentiality of the written communications between a lawyer and his client is not addressed at this place once again; in this respect, the above statements within Point 3.6.5. ("Respect for private and family life") are referred to.

3.6.8.1. Legal certainty

The principle of justice is at the pinnacle of the pyramid of legal norms. However, it cannot be observed in isolation, but must be appreciated in conjunction with the other leading principles of law, especially the principle of legal certainty: in case of conflict, "the principle of justice, however, must always be harmonised with the principle of legal certainty, which likewise is based on the requirements of justice and economy. These two principles must be so reconciled as to entail the minimum of sacrifice by persons as a whole within the Community".[130]

Consequently, the legal certainty is an integral part of the formal justice. The principle requires that the legal norms, which are relevant for answering a legal question, are already certain as regards substance, at least, as broad guidelines before the decision is made. This should be transparent and predictable, which results in the requirement of the predictability of the acts of the Community/Union as well as of the authorities of the Member States within the scope of application of the Community/Union law.[131] The legal subjects should be sure of their rights and, on this basis, should be in a position to make necessary arrangements.[132]

The principle of legal certainty manifests itself in several forms and contexts. Thus, for instance, unlawful beneficial administrative acts "in certain cases, in view of the vested rights, cannot be cancelled ex tunc", thus, with a retroactive effect.[133] The retroactive enactment of a regulation cannot impair the rights of persons, whose claims arose before the proclamation of the regulation.[134] Except for criminal law or similar cases (e.g., disciplinary procedures)[135], the prohibition on

---

130 Judgement of 13.7.1962, Klöckner und Hoesch, ibid.

131 Cf. Dieter Feger, Die Normsetzung auf dem Gebiet der Grundrechte in den Europäischen Gemeinschaften – Der Europäische Gerichtshof (EuGH) als Rechtsetzungsorgan, in: DÖV 1987, p. 322.

132 Judgement of 6.12.2001, Area Cova, Case T-196/99, EuGE 2001, II-3597, II-3631 et seqq.; judgement of 6.3.2003, Commission v Luxembourg, Case C-478/01, ECR 2003, I-2351, I-2366.

133 Judgement of 1.6.1961, Simon, Case 15/60, ECR 1961, 239, 259 et seq.; judgement of 13.7.1965, Lemmerz-Werke, Case 111/63, ECR 1965, 893, 911.

134 Judgement of 15.7.1964, van der Veen, Case 100/63, ECR 1964, 1219, 1233 et seq.

135 In these cases, the prohibition of "*nullum crimen sine lege*" and/or "*nulla poena sine lege*" strictly apply, cf. Article 7 ECHR.

retroactivity of burdensome regulations is, however, not absolute, but can be restricted for reasons of public interest; exceptions can be considered, if the object of the measure demands it, and the legitimate expectation of the persons concerned is taken into consideration.[136]

3.6.8.2. Protection of legitimate expectations

The principle of legal certainty is closely related to the principle of the protection of legitimate expectations; often both go hand in hand.[137] Tension exists between the legal certainty and the protection of legitimate expectations, on the one hand, and the principle of legality, on the other hand, so that by weighing the public interest against the private interests, which are at stake, it is to be ascertained, which of these principles outweigh in individual case.[138]

On the basis of the principle of the protection of legitimate expectations, which according to the case-law of the ECJ, in particular in the area of the protection of ownership, plays a significant role, the economic operators should be protected from a subsequent devaluation of the legal position acquired or arrangements undertaken. But such protection can arise only if the Community or an authority of the Member State had, due to their actions or omissions, created a situation of legitimate expectation within the scope of application of the Community law, on which the individuals could legitimately rely. Add to this as another condition that the guaranteed legal position was created in favour of the individual, which is not the case if the Community or the Member State concerned can amend the existing legal position, at any time, to the detriment of the parties involved, and a prudent economic operator has to anticipate such an amendment.[139] This conclusion im-

136 Judgement of 21.2.1991, Zuckerfabrik Süderdithmarschen, Cases C-143/88 and C-92/89, ECR 1991, I-415, I-548. In this connection, it is noted that the so-called "quasi-retroactive effect" (retrospectivity), i.e., the situation that a new rule is applied to the future effects of situations, which arose under the earlier rules, is not seen by the case-law of the ECJ or GC as an issue concerning retroactive problems (retroactivity): judgement of 6.12.2001, Area Cova, ibid.

137 Hans-Werner Rengeling/Peter Szczekalla, Grundrechte in der Europäischen Union – Charta der Grundrechte und allgemeine Rechtsgrundsätze, 2004, p. 450.

138 Judgement of 22.3.1961, SNUPAT, Cases 42/59 and 45/59, ECR 1961, 109, 172.

139 Judgement of 14.5.1975, CNTA, Case 74/74, ECR 1975, 533, 548 et seq.; judgement of 27.9.1979, Eridania, Case 230/78, ECR 1979, 2749, 2768 et seq.; judgement of 21.9.1983, Deutsche Milchkontor, Case 205-215/82, ECR 1983, 2633, 2664 et seq.; judgement of 19.5.1992, Mulder and Heinemann, Cases C-104/89 and C-37/90, ECR 1992, I-3061, para 13 et seq.; judgement of 15.4.1997, Irish Farmers Association, Case C-22/94, ECR 1997, I-1809, I-1839 et seq.

plies that, basically, no individual right to the continuance of an economic benefit, which was granted once, exists.[140]

To summarise the above, the preconditions for the occurrence of a situation of legitimate expectation under Community/Union law could be defined with the help of the following criteria:[141]

- existence of a position of legitimate expectation, which was created by the Community/Union or the Member States within the scope of application of the Community/Union law;
- protection-worthiness of the legitimate expectation in the sense that only the guaranteed legal positions, i.e., those, which could not be amended by the competent authorities within the scope of their discretion, enjoy the protection of legitimate expectations;
- weighing the individual interest against the Community/Union interests, i.e., the individual interest can be worthy of protection only if it outweighs.

3.6.8.3. Right to a hearing

The right to a fair trial ("*due process*") is a leading communitarian principle of procedural nature, which forms a necessary supplement to the general principles of the substantive Community/Union law. The relevant sources of the knowledge of law can be found in the provisions of the European Convention on Human Rights (Article 6: right to a fair trial; Article 13: right to an effective remedy), as well as in the constitutional orders of several EU Member States.[142] However, the question whether the right to a fair trial is a procedural fundamental right or rather a procedural right, which ranks as a fundamental right, may be left open.[143]

This law has, in particular, in its expression as the "right to a hearing",[144] unmistakably attained significant importance in the case-law of the ECJ. As such, it has to be observed not only in the proceedings before the Court of Justice itself, but also in the administrative proceedings before the Community/Union institutions and bodies. In such cases, it presupposes that "the undertakings concerned

---

140 Judgement of 6.12.2001, Area Cova, ibid., II- 3637 et seqq.

141 Cf. Hans-Werner Rengeling, Grundrechtsschutz in der Europäischen Gemeinschaft, 1993, p. 49.

142 E.g., Article 19(4) 1st sentence of the German Basic Law, which guarantees the recourse ("Rechtsweg") against all the acts of the public authorities.

143 Judgement of 29.6.1994, Fiskano, Case C-135/92, ECR 1994, I-2885, I-2909.

144 However, the French legal doctrine preferably uses the term "*droits de la défense*". This term has a broader semantic content as regards subject matter than that of the "right to a hearing", on the one hand, but, on the other hand, restricts the *ratione personae* protection to the rights of the defendant in the procedure.

must have been afforded the opportunity during the administrative procedure to make known their views on the truth and relevance of the facts and circumstances alleged and on the documents used". If such facts and circumstances cannot be imparted, for instance, for reasons of business confidentiality, they may not be taken into consideration, if the undertakings concerned would be constrained in their defence thereby.[145]

The right to a hearing includes the right of access to the file (access to the relevant documents) as an auxiliary preparatory right.[146]

3.6.8.4. Right against self-incrimination

The right against self-incrimination, in particular, to not be compelled to make a declaration against oneself, is, to some extent, the other side of the right to a hearing. A comparative overview of the constitutional orders of the Member States shows that very different provisions are applicable for the existence or the substance and scope of the right to silence in one's own case. The legal systems vary with regard to the circle of privileged persons (only natural persons or even legal persons), the type of procedure (only criminal proceedings, disciplinary proceedings and similar procedures or even disputes under private or administrative law), as well as the hierarchical ranking of the applicable prohibition norms (constitutional law or common law).

Against the background of this diversity of national provisions, the Court of Justice assumes a graduated protection under the Community law: It restricts the *ratione personae* to the natural persons; on the other hand, it resorts to the *ratione materiae* only within the course of criminal or comparable proceedings, excluding the procedures for sanctioning violations of economic nature, in particular, in the area of competition law.[147] In no case can a prohibition of self-incrimination be objected to in procedures, which exclusively relate to private law relationships, and could not lead to the imposition of criminal or administrative sanctions, even if the person concerned has to admit an infringement of the competition rules. The right to silence primarily serves "to protect an individual against measures of investigation ordered by public authorities to obtain his admission of the existence of conduct laying him open to administrative or criminal penalties".[148]

---

145 Judgement of 13.2.1979, Hoffmann – La Roche, Case 85/76, ECR 1979, 461, 511.

146 Cf. judgement of 19.2.1998, Eyckeler and Malt, Case T-42/96, EuGE 1998, II-401, II-425.

147 Judgement of 18.10.1989, Orkem v Commission, Case 374//87, ECR 1989, 3283, 3348 et seqq.

148 Judgement of 10.11.1993, Otto v Postbank, Case C-60/92, ECR 1993, I-5686, I-5711 et seq.

Consequently, undertakings in antitrust proceedings before the Commission have the benefit of only conditional protection with regard to a possible obligation to incriminate themselves. However, the judicature of the ECJ in no case deprives these persons of any protection. Thus, the Commission may not ask an undertaking to admit infringements, which it is incumbent upon the Commission to prove.[149]

3.6.8.5. The ne bis in idem principle

Sanctions in Community/Union disciplinary proceedings or administrative penalty proceedings fall under the maxim "*ne bis in idem*" (prohibition of double jeopardy),[150] which was originally developed for the criminal proceedings.

The *ne bis in idem* principle is, however, not directly applicable in the relationship of the sanctions according to Community/Union law with those of the national law for violation of competition rules, because the Community/Union law and the national law constitute two interdependent legal circles, which are, nevertheless, separated from each other. However, it follows from the close interdependence that the Commission, in its capacity as the Community/Union competition authority, has to, in determining the amount of the fine to be imposed under Community/Union law, take into account the sanctions which were already imposed for the same circumstances in a Member State on the basis of the national law.[151]

It is to be noted that the *ne bis in idem* principle does not rule out that, besides a conviction in a criminal proceeding (or an administrative penalty proceeding respectively), claims for damages under civil law are asserted.[152]

---

149 Judgement of 18.10.1989, Orkem v Commission, Case 374/87, ibid., 3351.

150 Judgement of 15.3.1967, Gutmann, Cases 18/65 and 35/65, ECR 1967, 79, 88.

151 Judgement of 13.2.1969, Walt Wilhelm and others v Bundeskartellamt, Case 14/68, ECR 1969, 1, 15; judgement of 14.12.1972, Boehringer v Commission, Case 7/72, ECR 1972, 1280, 1290.

152 Judgement of 11.2.2003, Gözütok and Brügge, Cases C-187/01 and C-385/01, ECR 2003, I-1345, I-1395.

4. From the case-law of the ECJ to the European Charter of Fundamental Rights

Although the judicial case-law can meet the requirements of specific justice in individual cases, however, cannot replace any cross-case, comprehensive codification. The Community institutions and the EU Member States were painfully aware of it, at the latest, in the course of the trends towards a constitutionalisation of the European Union. This process gave reasons to think about adopting a single, autonomous catalogue of fundamental rights, which led to the establishment and mandating of a European Convention on Fundamental Rights and, as a result of the work of this Convention, to the final proclamation of the so-called "Charter of Fundamental Rights".

The process of emergence, the legal nature and the substance (essential content) of the Charter of Fundamental Rights will be presented in the following.

4.1. Process of emergence of the Charter of Fundamental Rights[153]

The European Council, at its meeting in Cologne on 4 June 1999, advocated the consolidation of fundamental rights, which are, or should be, applicable at the level of the European Union, in a charter, in order to meet the growing need for the codification and legitimation at the European level.[154] For this purpose, a Convention, under the chairmanship of the former German President Roman Herzog, comprising 64 members, was established with the task to elaborate a Charter of Fundamental Rights. The codification should firstly reflect the already applicable rights, which are sporadically contained in the Treaties or arise from the case-law of the ECJ, and make them visible to the people. But even the innovative fundamental rights, which are adapted to the recent developments of the Union, should

153 On this point, see, in general: Gráinne de Búrca, The Drafting of the European Union Charter of Fundamental Rights, in: ELR 2001, p. 126.

154 Presidency conclusions of the Cologne European Council, 3. and 4.6.1999, Annex IV.

be enshrined in the Charter, which, in addition to the fundamental liberal civil rights, should also secure the fundamental social rights.[155]

Owing to the different legal traditions of the Member States and the scepticism against a collectively written catalogue of fundamental rights, and due to the different concepts of content and effect of the formulated fundamental rights, fundamental principles and values, the working group had, in no way, the prospect of a successful result in the beginning. Another stumbling block was the concern that due to the wording of the fundamental rights and fundamental principles, new competences could arise for the Union, and the Member States could lose additional national responsibilities.

The Charter was elaborated in the course of the constitutionalisation of the European Union, which was strived for at that time, and on 7.12.2000, was adopted in the form of a solemn, but non-binding proclamation by the European Council and the Community institutions.

4.2. Legal nature of the Charter of Fundamental Rights prior to the Lisbon Treaty[156]

From the outset, the concurrent political will of all the forces involved was, however, not to leave the non-binding proclamation at that, but to create a binding legislative act as an integral part of the primary Union law.

---

155 Cf. Hans D. Jarass, EU-Grundrechte, 2005, p. 9. See also Resolution A5-0064/2000 of the European Parliament on the elaboration of a Charter of Fundamental Rights of the European Union: minutes of the plenary session of 16.3.2000; Resolution B5-767/2000 of the European Parliament on the Charter of Fundamental Rights: minutes of the plenary session of 3.10.2000.

156 On this point, see, in general: Commission of the European Communities, Communication from the Commission on the legal nature of the Charter of Fundamental Rights of the European Union, Brussels, 11.10.2000, COM (2000) 644 final; Siegbert Alber, Die Selbstbindung der europäischen Organe an die Europäische Charta der Grundrechte, in: EuGRZ 2001, p. 349; Herta Däubler-Gmelin, Eine europäische Charta der Grundrechte – Beitrag zur gemeinsamen Identität, in: EuZW 2000, p. 1; Dirk Ehlers, European Fundamental Rights and Freedoms, 2007; Meinhard Hilf, Ein Grundrechtskatalog für die Europäische Gemeinschaft, in: EuR 1991, p. 19; Andrea Iber, Der Status der Grundrechtscharta im Gemeinschaftsrecht – Derzeitige Verbindlichkeit und Zukunftsperspektiven der Charta – insbesondere im Verfassungskonvent, in: ZEuS 2002, p. 483; Mathias H. Knecht, Die Charta der Grundrechte der Europäischen Union: Eine Würdigung der Entstehung und rechtsvergleichende grundrechtsdogmatische Analyse, 2005; Siegfried Magiera, Die Grundrechtecharta der Europäischen Union, in: DÖV 2000, p. 1017; Matthias Mahlmann, Die Grundrechtecharta der Europäischen Union, in: ZEuS 2000, p. 419; Martin Nettesheim, Die

Accordingly, already in the drafting stage, the Charter was treated "as though" it will be an integral part of a Union's Constitution in future. This "as though" approach is corroborated by the General Provisions (Chapter VII of the text), which would have been superfluous, had the Charter been conceived only as a solemn political declaration. On the other hand, the European Charter of Fundamental Rights, originally, was neither primary nor secondary Community law, because it was not adopted in a formal procedure enshrined in the Treaties. However, this document served from the beginning as an important reference text for the interpretation of the Community law by the ECJ, which ascribed it, at least, indirect legal relevance[157] in the sense that the fundamental rights guaranteed and protected therein align and interweave the European legal order altogether.[158] This is a feature of a source of the knowledge of communitarian law.[159]

Even if several areas of the Charter of Fundamental Rights reflect the already existing general principles of law, the Charter was at the outset a non-binding proclamation, which although promised a significant gain in transparency for the legal subjects, the function of which, however, did not go beyond a mere guidance

---

Charta der Grundrechte der Europäischen Union: Eine verfassungstheoretische Kritik, in: Integration, 2002, p. 35; Eckhardt Pache, Die Europäische Grundrechtscharta – ein Rückschritt für den Grundrechtsschutz in Europa?, in: EuR 2001, p. 475; Walter Pauly, Strukturfragen des unionsrechtlichen Grundrechtsschutzes, in: EuR 1998, p. 242; Ingolf Pernice, Gemeinschaftsverfassung und Grundrechtsschutz – Grundlagen, Bestand, Perspektiven, in: NJW 1990, p. 2409; idem, Eine Grundrechte – Charta für die Europäische Union, in: DVBl 2000, p. 847; Nina Philippi, Die Charta der Grundrechte der Europäischen Union, 2002, Georg J. Schmittmann, Rechte und Grundsätze in der Grundrechtecharta, 2007; Thomas Schmitz, Die Grundrechtecharta als Teil der Verfassung der Europäischen Union, in: EuR 2004, p. 691; Albrecht Weber, Die Europäische Grundrechtscharta – auf dem Weg zu einer europäischen Verfassung, in: NJW 2000, p. 537; idem, Charta der Grundrechte der Europäischen Union, 2002.

157 Cf. Josef Franz Lindner, Grundrechtsschutz gegen gemeinschaftsrechtliche Öffnungsklauseln – zugleich ein Beitrag zum Anwendungsbereich der EU-Grundrechte, in: EuZW 2007, p. 71.

158 Cf. Rudolf Streinz, in: idem (editor), EUV/EGV–Vertrag über die Europäische Union und Vertrag zur Gründung der Europäischen Gemeinschaft, 2003, p. 2573 et seq. Cf. Erhard Denninger, Menschenrechte und Staatsaufgaben – ein europäisches Thema, in: JZ 1996, p. 585, 587.

159 Although the ECJ and/or the CFI have, in their judgements, repeatedly referred to the Charter of Fundamental Rights (thus, for instance, the judgement of 29.4.2004, Tokai Carbon and others v Commission, Cases T-236/01, T-239/01, T-244/01 to 246/01, T-251/01 and T-252/01, EuGE 2004, II-1181, II-1238, para 119; judgement of 8.7.2004, JFE Engineering and others v Commission, Cases T-67/00, T-68/00, T-71/00, and T-78/00, EuGE 2004, II-2501, II-2582, para 178), however, insofar evident, have not relied on the Charter until now as the law, which is decisive for the procedures (cf. judgement of 6.11.2003, Lindqvist, Case C-101/01, ECR 2003, I-12971, I-13020 et seqq., para 72 et seqq.)

as a secondary source of law. The attempt to integrate the Charter into the "Treaty establishing a Constitution for Europe" (Constitutional Treaty) failed,[160] and only the Lisbon Reform Treaty of 13.12.2007, which is in force since 1.12.2009, transformed the Charter from a mere solemn, but non-binding proclamation into a mandatory instrument of primary Union law by declaring it, through a cross-reference, to be legally binding, and in fact, equalling the rank of Union Treaty law (Article 6(1) 1st sentence TEU in the version of the Treaty of Lisbon).[161]

4.3. Contents of the Charter of Fundamental Rights

4.3.1. Preliminary remark and overview

The Charter, which was solemnly proclaimed on 7.12.2000, consists of 54 articles, which are divided into seven chapters: I – "Dignity"; II – "Freedoms"; III – "Equality"; IV – "Solidarity"; V – "Citizens' Rights"; VI – "Justice"; VII – "General Provisions".

The preamble[162] consists of seven paragraphs, the first of which commits to a peaceful future based on common values within the scope of an ever closer Union.

The subsequent paragraph places the fundamental values of the Union in the foreground. Although it contains no explicit reference to God, however, is based on the spiritual and moral heritage of the peoples of Europe, which also enshrines their religious traditions. In this context, priority has also been given to the indivisible, universal values of human dignity, freedom, equality and solidarity.

The subsequent paragraphs corroborate and specify the aforementioned common values, and integrate them into the economic and social objectives of the Union. The necessity of adopting one's own Charter of Fundamental Rights is made clear in the fourth paragraph of the preamble:

---

160 Due to the negative outcome of the referendums in France and the Netherlands, concerning the Constitutional Treaty.

161 The Treaty of Lisbon, according to its final provisions, required the ratification by all EU Member States so as to be able to come into force. After the negative outcome of the first plebiscite in Ireland, this Member State could only ratify the Treaty on the basis of a second, successful referendum, which was held on 2.10.2009.

162 On this point, see: Christian Busse, Eine kritische Würdigung der Präambel der Europäischen Grundrechtecharta, in: EuGRZ 2002, p. 559.

"...it is necessary to strengthen the protection of fundamental rights in the light of changes in society, social progress and scientific and technological developments by making those rights more visible in a Charter."

The provisions of the Charter are mostly self-executing, i.e., they have been drafted so clearly and absolutely that they would be directly applicable in the event the Charter becomes legally binding. Specific provisions are restricted to objective institutional guarantees; however, they do not create any subjective rights in favour of the individuals concerned. Still other provisions of the Charter enshrine non-binding policy clauses and provisions (soft-law) or purely political objectives, the realisation of which depends on the financial or general economic and political conditions. Another differentiation can be made between "everyone's rights", i.e., the rights, which benefit not just the Union's citizens, and the "Union's citizens' rights", i.e., rights, which are linked to the citizenship of the Union.

The "classic" rights could be compared with the rights in the "modern" world. For the purpose of explanation, it is stated that – as it arises from the General Provisions (Chapter VII, Articles 51-54) of the Charter – this instrument does not create a completely new fundamental rights system, but rather intends to retain and enhance the existing fundamental rights (cf., in particular, the reference to the European Convention on Human Rights in Articles 52(3), 53 of the Charter). Although the general provisions do not explicitly refer to the judicature of the ECJ, it is predominantly assumed that the Charter primarily codifies this case-law, which is the foundation and central pillar of the rights under the Charter, and which forms its most important source for the interpretation. This finding, however, does not prevent the Charter from providing new "modern" rights, by further developing the law, which transcend the case-law acquis of the ECJ.

A schematic overview of the Chapters and Articles of the European Charter of Fundamental Rights is presented in the following on the basis of the official titles.

Structure of the European Charter of Fundamental Rights

Preamble

Chapter I: Dignity

- Article 1: Human dignity
- Article 2: Right to life
- Article 3: Right to the integrity of the person
- Article 4: Prohibition of torture and inhuman or degrading treatment or punishment
- Article 5: Prohibition of slavery and forced labour

Chapter II: Freedoms

- Article 6: Right to liberty and security
- Article 7: Respect for private and family life
- Article 8: Protection of personal data
- Article 9: Right to marry and right to found a family
- Article 10: Freedom of thought, conscience and religion
- Article 11: Freedom of expression and information
- Article 12: Freedom of assembly and of association
- Article 13: Freedom of the arts and sciences
- Article 14: Right to education
- Article 15: Freedom to choose an occupation and right to engage in work
- Article 16: Freedom to conduct a business
- Article 17: Right to property
- Article 18: Right to asylum
- Article 19: Protection in the event of removal, expulsion or extradition

Chapter III: Equality

- Article 20: Equality before the law
- Article 21: Non-discrimination

- Article 22: Cultural, religious and linguistic diversity
- Article 23: Equality between men and women
- Article 24: The rights of the child
- Article 25: The rights of the elderly
- Article 26: Integration of persons with disabilities

Chapter IV: Solidarity

- Article 27: Workers' right to information and consultation within the undertaking
- Article 28: Right of collective bargaining and action
- Article 29: Right of access to placement services
- Article 30: Protection in the event of unjustified dismissal
- Article 31: Fair and just working conditions
- Article 32: Prohibition of child labour and protection of young people at work
- Article 33: Family and professional life
- Article 34: Social security and social assistance
- Article 35: Health care
- Article 36: Access to services of general economic interest
- Article 37: Environmental protection
- Article 38: Consumer protection

Chapter V: Citizens' Rights

- Article 39: Right to vote and to stand as a candidate at elections to the European Parliament
- Article 40: Right to vote and to stand as a candidate at municipal elections
- Article 41: Right to good administration
- Article 42: Right of access to documents
- Article 43: Ombudsman
- Article 44: Right to petition
- Article 45: Freedom of movement and of residence
- Article 46: Diplomatic and consular protection

Chapter VI: Justice

- Article 47: Right to an effective remedy and to a fair trial
- Article 48: Presumption of innocence and right of defence
- Article 49: Principles of legality and proportionality of criminal offences and penalties
- Article 50: Right not to be tried or punished twice in criminal proceedings for the same criminal offence

Chapter VII: General Provisions

- Article 51: Scope
- Article 52: Scope of guaranteed rights
- Article 53: Level of protection
- Article 54: Prohibition of abuse of rights

4.3.2. Human dignity

The Charter of Fundamental Rights devotes a separate chapter to the human dignity at a very prominent place, right at the beginning of the text of the Charter (Chapter I). Already in the preamble, it is declared that the human dignity is an indivisible and universal value. It constitutes "the real basis of fundamental rights"[163]. Thereby, on the one hand, it is a highest constitutional principle (similar to that in Article 1(1) of the German Basic Law)[164], which spreads to the subsequent fundamental rights and exaggerates them, on the other hand, it is an independent fundamental right, which can be cited as an individual rule.[165]

Both the decisive aspects of the guarantee of human dignity, viz., aspects of defence and protection,[166] are pointed out at the key position (Article 1): "Human

163 Explanations relating to the Charter of Fundamental Rights of 14.12.2007, OJ. 2007, C 303/17.

164 In this connection, see Martin Borowsky, in: Jürgen Meyer, Kommentar zur Charta der Grundrechte der Europäischen Union, 2nd edition 2006, before Chapter I, para 1a; Article 1, para 27.

165 In this connection, probably the judgements of the ECJ of 30.4.1996, P v S and Cornwall County Council, Case C-13/94, ECJ 1996, I-2143, I-2165; judgement of 9.10.2001, Netherlands v Parliament and Council, Case C-377/98, ECR 2001, I-7079, 7168 et seqq.

166 Cf. Christian Calliess, Die Charta der Grundrechte der Europäischen Union – Fragen der Konzeption, Kompetenz und Verbindlichkeit, EuZW 2001, p. 261, 263.

dignity is inviolable. It must be respected and protected". This dual guarantee represents the most important value judgement of the Charter of Fundamental Rights.[167] It constitutes the real basis and the concept of the subsequent fundamental rights[168], inasmuch as it serves not only to provide a defence against State interventions, but also contains the obligation of the State authorities to protect against infringements on the part of the third parties.[169] Restrictions on the guarantee of human dignity are ruled out because human dignity belongs to the inviolable substance of the fundamental rights (cf. Article 52(1) Charter of Fundamental Rights).

Article 2 of the Charter of Fundamental Rights affirms the protection of life, including the prohibition of death penalty. Consequently, this prohibition constitutes an absolute limit of restrictions on the right to life.[170] Giving a signal to the whole world, it was included in the Charter, although the EU Member States had already recognised the prohibition with the ratification of the 6th Additional Protocol to the European Convention on Human Rights. In this connection, the question has been raised in the literature on various occasions, whether the prohibition of death penalty has only a symbolic character in the Charter of Fundamental Rights because the Union lacks the competence to impose and enforce the death penalty.[171] This question should be answered in the negative for two reasons: Firstly, it is pointed out that even if the Union, at the present time, does not have the appropriate competences in the area of criminal law, without the prohibition of death penalty, the Union could be assigned such competences in future, thus, for instance, within the scope of the so-called third pillar (police and judicial cooperation in criminal matters). It is, moreover, pointed out that the Charter is valid not only for the institutions and bodies of the Union, but also for the Member States when implementing the Union law (cf. Article 51(1) Charter of Fundamental Rights). Without the prohibition of death penalty in the Charter, it would not be guaranteed, with absolute legal certainty, that the Member States can, in no case, adopt the means of the death penalty when sanctioning the violations of the Community/Union law.

---

167 Cf. Martin Borowsky, ibid., Article 1, para 39.

168 Dorothee von Arnim, Der Standort der EU-Grundrechtecharta in der Grundrechtsarchitektur Europas, Dissertation, Würzburg 2006, p. 128. Also, Georg J. Schmittmann, Rechte und Grundsätze in der Grundrechtecharta, 2007, p. 99, and OJ. 2004, C 310/420 (Explanations, Article 1).

169 Nina Philippi, Die Charta der Grundrechte der Europäischen Union, 2002, p. 21.

170 Cf. Hans D. Jarass, EU-Grundrechte, ibid., p. 120.

171 Cf. Udo Ostermann, Entwicklung und gegenwärtiger Stand der europäischen Grundrechte nach der Rechtsprechung des Europäischen Gerichtshofs sowie des Gerichts erster Instanz, ibid., p. 166.

Article 3 guarantees the right to respect for physical and mental integrity; Article 4 prohibits the torture or inhuman or degrading treatment or punishment, and Article 5 prohibits slavery, forced labour and trafficking in human beings.

Article 3(2) deserves a particular mention, which, with the ethical code of conduct in the field of "medicine and biology", paves the way for the modern fundamental rights, according to which the integrity of the person should be protected also in the context of constant advancements in medicine and biology. Thereby, for instance, the prohibition of eugenic practices (Article 3(2), second indent) or the prohibition of the reproductive cloning of human beings (Article 3(2), fourth indent), thus, practices, which are hotly debated of late, are in the foreground.[172] For this reason, the mentioned provisions, which are modelled on the European Council's Convention on Human Rights and Biomedicine of 1998, have been accorded a signalling effect in view of the challenges of the modern biotechnology.

The prohibition of trafficking in human beings (Article 5(3)) seems to have already been enshrined in the guarantee of human dignity. The fact that it is, nevertheless, mentioned separately in the Charter, should be seen against the background that the Union explicitly condemns and declares a battle against the newer developments in the area of organised crime, such as, e.g., smuggling and trafficking of human beings for the purpose of sexual exploitation.[173]

4.3.3. Freedoms

Chapter II of the Charter lists several freedoms, beginning with the general commitment to a "right to liberty and security" (Article 6). Thereby, the classic liberal freedoms, which are already enshrined in the European Convention on Human Rights, are in the foreground.[174] These are to be highlighted in this regard: respect for private and family life (Article 7), right to marry and right to found a family (Article 9), freedom of thought, conscience and religion (Article 10), freedom of expression and information (Article 11), as well as the freedom of assembly and of association (Article 12).

With regard to the respect for private and family life (Article 7), it is to be noted that this provision is synonymous with Article 8 of ECHR, so that according to Article 52(3) of the Charter of Fundamental Rights, even the limitations of

172 Cf. Christian Calliess, ibid. See also: Explanations relating to the Charter of Fundamental Rights of 14.12.2007, OJ. 2007, C 303/18.

173 On this point, see: Explanations relating to the Charter of Fundamental Rights of 14.12.2007, OJ. 2007, C 303/19. Cf. also Dorothee von Arnim, ibid., p. 129.

174 On this point, see: Explanations relating to the Charter of Fundamental Rights of 14.12.2007, OJ. 2007, C 303/19 et seq.

Article 8(2) ECHR can apply. Accordingly, the interventions in the exercise of this right are permissible only if they are in accordance with the law, and represent a measure, which is necessary in a democratic society, among other things, for the national security, public peace and order or for the protection of rights and freedoms of others. According to the recent case-law of the ECJ, the term "private life" must not be interpreted restrictively, and must not fundamentally exclude the activities of a professional nature.[175] Even the right to marry and the right to found a family (Article 9 of the Charter) are derived from the European Convention on Human Rights (Article 12), however, differ from its relevant provisions in that "men and women" are not explicitly referred to, but simply a reference has been made to the "national laws governing the exercise of these rights". Therewith, it has been left to the fundamental judgement of the national legislator, whether it recognises the same-sex partnerships as the framework for founding a family.[176]

Article 10 of the Charter pertaining to the freedom of thought, conscience and religion corresponds almost word-for-word with Article 9(1) of the ECHR. According to that, restrictions could arise from Article 9(2) ECHR: They must be in accordance with the law and necessary in a democratic society. The right to conscientious objection, which is enshrined in Article 10(2) of the Charter, is new; it is *ius imperfectum*, inasmuch as it refers to the national laws for the exercise of this right.

Article 11 of the Charter, which guarantees the freedom of expression and information, is based largely on the model of Article 10 of the ECHR. The rights guaranteed as such reflect the relevance of the formation of public opinion and free communication. In the light of the case-law of the ECJ, they form an essential foundation of a democratic society, and are an important precondition for its progress and for the development of each individual person.[177] Restrictions are permissible, if they are prescribed by law and are necessary in a democratic society.[178]

A right to the freedom of assembly and of association (Article 12 of the Charter), within the scope of which, in particular, the freedom of trade union association and the right to join political parties should be highlighted, is based on Article 11 of the ECHR.

---

175 Judgement of 20.5.2003, Rechnungshof v Österreichischer Rundfunk, Cases C 465/00, C-138/01 and C-139/01, ECR 2003, I-4989, I-5043.

176 Explanations relating to the Charter of Fundamental Rights of 14.12.2007, OJ. 2007, C 303/21. Cf. Dorothee von Arnim, ibid., p. 131; Peter J. Tettinger, Die Charta der Grundrechte der Europäischen Union, in: NJW 2001, p. 1010, 1012 et seq.

177 Judgement of 6.3.2001, Connolly v Commission, Case C-274/99 P, ECR 2001, I-1611, I-1675 et seq.

178 Judgement of 26.6.1997, Familiapress, Case C-368/95, ECR 1997, I-3689, I-3717.

A present-day right to freedom, the protection of personal data, is enshrined in Article 8 of the Charter. This provision is not derived from the ECHR, but is modelled on (ex-)Article 286 of the TEC and the communitarian Data Protection Directive 95/46/EC,[179] the basic messages of which are thus elevated to the rank of fundamental rights. Article 8(1) substantiates the right of every person to the protection of personal data concerning him or her.; Paragraph 2, 1st sentence of this Article presupposes the consent of the person concerned or some other "legitimate basis laid down by law" as a condition for the data-processing. Paragraph 2, 2nd sentence substantiates the right of every person to access to, and rectification of the data concerning them. The petitum expressed by several parties, to grant the person concerned a right to appeal to a Union Data Protection Supervisor, however, has not been complied with until now.[180]

Altogether, the data protection stipulated under Article 8 of the Charter comes close to a fundamental right of self-determination over personal data, as the German Constitutional Court has derived from Article 2(1) in conjunction with Article 1(1) of the German Basic Law[181].

The protection of arts and scientific research, including the academic freedom (Article 13 of the Charter), is likewise not enshrined in the ECHR. The right to education and the access to vocational and continuing training are akin to it. If educational institutions exist in a Member State, these must be open to everyone in terms of non-discriminatory access; moreover, the participation in compulsory education must be facilitated free of cost, whereby socio-economic discriminations should be avoided in the educational sector (Article 14 of the Charter).

This is followed by the right to engage in work and to pursue a freely chosen occupation (Article 15 of the Charter), further followed by the freedom to conduct a business (Article 16 of the Charter):

---

179 Directive 95/46/EC of the European Parliament and of the Council of 24.10.1995 on the protection of individuals with regard to the processing of personal data and on the free movement of such data, OJ. 1995, L 281/31. On this point, see: judgement of 6.11.2003, Lindqvist, Case C-101/01, ECR 2003, I-12971, I-12982.

180 On the issue of the protection of personal data see, in general: Christoph Grabenwarter, Die Charta der Grundrechte für die Europäische Union, in: DVBl. 2001, p. 1, 4; Matthias Mahlmann, Die Grundrechtecharta der Europäischen Union, in: ZEuS 2000, p. 419, 435. According to Article 286(1) TEC (replaced by Article 16 TFEU and Article 39 TEU), from 1.1.1999, the Community acts on the protection of individuals with regard to the processing and the free movement of personal data shall apply to the institutions and bodies of the Community. According to Para 2 of this Article, the Council shall establish an independent supervisory body responsible for monitoring the application of such Community acts to Community institutions and bodies.

181 Cf. BVerfGE vol. 65, p. 1, 41 et seqq.

Article 15 enshrines a comprehensive fundamental right to choose an occupation, both in the form of career choices, as well as freedom of occupational practice (Paragraph 1). In addition, – for the citizens of the Union – their right to look for a job, subordinate employment, the freedom of establishment and the freedom to provide services are specified (Paragraph 2).

Article 16, which especially enshrines the right to independent, entrepreneurial activities, supplements Article 15, which focuses on the rights of the subordinate employees. The separate reference to the freedom to conduct a business is a novelty, which was not considered in any international human rights catalogue until now. Therewith, the modern and innovative character of the European Charter of Fundamental Rights is clearly underlined once again. Admittedly, a detailed separation of both the relevant articles (15 and 16) may be dispensable in the practical application of law, since the ECJ has already attached fundamental relevance even to the freedom to conduct a business.[182]

Articles 15 and 16 do not substantiate any right to engage in work and/or freedom to conduct a business in terms of finding an appropriate job and, consequently, do not create any subjective right to an employment in order to secure the means of subsistence. Such a right could not be granted in a system of free market economy. On the contrary, the obligation of the State, in its capacity as the guarantor, restricts to that it may not take active measures by which anyone is prevented from commencing employment or taking up a profession.[183]

It needs to be emphasised that the Charter explicitly recognises neither a general right to free personal development nor a general freedom of action. However, these general rights may be deducible, at least partially, from Article 7 of the Charter (respect for private life).[184] The right to liberty and security (Article 6) is, in any case, not relevant because it does not cover the general freedom of action, but only aims at the freedom of physical movement, in particular, the protection against unlawful detention and imprisonment ("*habeas corpus*").[185]

A comprehensive protection of property is provided under Article 17 of the Charter. This provision, together with the provisions concerning the freedom to choose an occupation and the freedom to conduct a business, forms the backbone

182 Thus, for example, the judgement of 30.7.1996, Bosphorus, Case C-84/95, ECR 1996, I-3953, I-3985.

183 Cf. Jürgen Meyer/Markus Engels, Aufnahme von sozialen Grundrechten in die europäische Grundrechtecharta?, in: ZRP 2000, p. 368, 370.

184 Cf. Siegfried Magiera, Die Grundrechtecharta der Europäischen Union, in: DÖV 2000, p. 1017, 1025.

185 On this point, see: Explanations relating to the Charter of Fundamental Rights of 14.12.2007, OJ. 2007, C 303/19 et seq. Cf. Norbert Bernsdorff, in: Jürgen Meyer, Kommentar zur Charta der Grundrechte der Europäischen Union, ibid., Article 6, para 10 et seqq.

of the fundamental economic rights of the Charter. According to it, everyone has the right, "to own, use, dispose of and bequeath his or her lawfully acquired possessions. No one may be deprived of his or her possessions, except in the public interest and in the cases and under the conditions provided for by law, subject to fair compensation being paid in good time for their loss. The use of property may be regulated by law in so far as is necessary for the general interest" (Article 17(1)).[186] Therefore, the protection of property focuses on the use and disposal of the lawfully acquired possessions, whereupon a formal expropriation within the meaning of Article 17(1), 2nd sentence is spoken of, if the ownership is transferred to the State or a third party. However, unlike, for instance, under Article 14(2) of the German Basic Law, no commitment to a social obligation of the ownership can be found in the Charter of Fundamental Rights.[187]

Both the concluding articles of Chapter II of the Charter are dedicated to specific provisions on the right to asylum (Article 18) and on the protection in the event of removal, expulsion or extradition (Article 19). The asylum is guaranteed in the light of the relevant provisions under the International and Community law, in particular, with due respect for the rules of the Geneva Convention of 28.7.1951, the Protocol of 31.1.1967 relating to the status of refugees and in accordance with the Treaty establishing the European Community. In this connection, it is contentious whether Article 18 of the Charter provides a subjective individual right to asylum for those fleeing political persecution.[188] The protection in the event of removal, expulsion or extradition, on the other hand, comprises, in particular, everyone's right not to be transferred to a State where there is a threat of death penalty, torture or other inhuman or degrading treatment or punishment.

---

186 According to the leading judgement of the ECJ in the case "Hauer" (see Point 3.6.2. above), the interventions in the right of ownership are possible at two levels of intensity: a) as mere usage restrictions resulting from the social obligations of property ownership (when other usage options of substantial importance remain with the rights-holder); the mere restriction on exercising the right to property can be justified by the reasonable considerations of the general public interest; b) as expropriation, i.e., as complete or extensive deprivation of property; an expropriation can be justified only for compelling reasons of general public interest and only against compensation: judgement of 13.12.1979, Hauer, Case 44/79, ECR 1979, 3727, 3746; cf. also judgement of 13.7.1989, Wachauf, Case 5/88, ECR 1989, 2609, 2639.

187 Cf. Matthias Mahlmann, Die Grundrechtecharta der Europäischen Union, ibid., p. 428.

188 In the negative: Norbert Bernsdorff, in: Jürgen Meyer, Kommentar zur Charta der Grundrechte der Europäischen Union, ibid., Article 18, para 11.

4.3.4. *Equality*

On the basis of the basic principle of "equality before the law" (Article 20), Chapter III enshrines various rights to equality and non-discrimination in seven articles, which with regard to their scope and specificity transcend Article 14 of the ECHR and probably even the corresponding provisions under the constitutions of most of the Member States.

The definition of the general principle of equality (Article 20) is fundamentally characterised by the above-mentioned case-law of the ECJ; it can be referred to at this place.[189] This general principle of equality is specified in greater detail, first and foremost, by the prohibitions on discrimination under Articles 21 and 23.

Article 21(1) of the Charter categorically prohibits "any discrimination based on any ground such as sex, race, colour, ethnic or social origin, genetic features, language, religion or belief, political or any other opinion, membership of a national minority, property, birth, disability, age or sexual orientation". This provision is, in turn, supplemented by a prohibition of "any discrimination on grounds of nationality" within the scope of application of the EC and EU Treaties. The latter prohibition (Article 21(2) of the Charter), which with regard to its nature is applicable only for the discrimination of the citizens of the Union, is modelled on Article 12(1) TEC (now: Article 18(1) TFEU). However, third country nationals could likewise have a right to equal treatment connected with the freedom to choose an occupation.[190]

A special prohibition of discrimination relates to – going beyond Article 141 TEC (now: Article 157 TFEU) – the equality between men and women, which must be ensured in all areas, including employment, work and pay (Article 23(1)),

---

189 Cf. the definition of the general principle of equality developed by the ECJ, whereupon "comparable situations should not be treated differently, unless the different treatment is objectively justified": judgement of 19.10.1977, "Quellmehl", Case 117/76 and 16/77, ECR 1977, 1753, 1770 et seq.; judgement of 19.10.1977, "Maisgritz", Case 124/76 and 20/77, ECR 1977, 1795, 1812 et seq.) Accordingly, it should be examined, as a first step, whether the respective situations are similar to each other with regard to the relevant criteria, i.e., are comparable. If it is affirmed, but, nevertheless, a different treatment is given, then, in a further step, the objective justification of the differentiation should be examined. In this connection, the ECJ, in its recent judicature, focuses on whether, in consideration of the principle of proportionality, an objective reason of considerable significance is given, which comes into consideration as the criterion for justification: judgement of 11.1.2000, Kreil, Case 285/98, ECR 2000, I-69, I-105; judgement of 13.4.2000, Karlsson, Case C-292/97, ECR 2000, I-2737, I-2777.

190 Cf. Article 15(3) of the Charter: "nationals of third countries who are authorised to work in the territories of the Member States are entitled to working conditions equivalent to those of citizens of the Union".

whereupon, however, it must be specified that the principle of equality shall not prevent the maintenance or adoption of measures providing for specific advantages in favour of the under-represented sex (so-called "positive discrimination", Article 23(2)).

With regard to the other four articles under Chapter III (Articles 22, 24-26), their assignment to the intrinsic equality rights can raise concerns:

Article 22 guarantees the respect for cultural, religious and linguistic diversity. It enshrines a commitment to "unity in diversity", however, without granting explicit subjective rights, such as the national minority rights.[191] Moreover, there would have been no need for this article because the key concepts of culture, religion and language have already been covered, directly or indirectly, by the precedents of the comprehensive prohibition of discrimination under Article 21. The independent function of Article 22 is, at the most, in elucidating that Europe is characterised by the diversity of different cultures. This diversity should preferably be retained, and the cultural homogenising tendencies should be countervailed.

Even the further three articles under Chapter III, which are devoted to the rights of the child (Article 24), the rights of the elderly (Article 25) and the integration of persons with disabilities (Article 26), only touch upon the periphery of the equality rights. They do not focus especially on equal treatment, rather primarily aim at the positive protection and support measures by which the natural disadvantages should be counterbalanced.

Article 24 concerning the rights of the child, in particular the right to protection and care, traces back to the United Nation Convention on the Rights of the Child.[192]

Children have a right to freedom of expression; their views on matters, which concern them, should be taken into consideration in accordance with their age and maturity. In all actions relating to children, the child's best interests must be a primary consideration. Moreover, the children have the right to maintain on a regular basis a personal relationship and direct contact with both his or her parents, unless that is contrary to his or her interests. Consequently, the beneficiaries of the fundamental right under this article are children, fundamental rights' addressees,

---

191 Nina Philippi, ibid., p. 24; Sven Hölscheidt, in: Jürgen Meyer, Kommentar zur Charta der Grundrechte der Europäischen Union, ibid., Article 22, para 16; Thorsten Kingreen, in: Christian Callies/Matthias Ruffert, EUV/EGV. Das Verfassungsrecht der Europäischen Union mit Europäischer Grundrechtecharta, Kommentar, 3rd edition, 2007, Article 22, para 2.

192 See: Explanations relating to the Charter of Fundamental Rights of 14.12.2007, OJ. 2007, C 303/25.

among others, are the citizens concerned, i.e., Article 24 partially displays a direct horizontal effect.[193]

Article 25 recognises a right of the elderly to lead a life of dignity and independence and to participate in social and cultural life. Therewith, – extending beyond the general prohibition of discrimination, among others, on grounds of age (Article 21(1)) – the right to active participation in political life is also covered.

Chapter III of the Charter is rounded off with Article 26 ("integration of persons with disabilities"). Under this provision, the Union commits to a right of persons with disabilities to benefit from measures designed to ensure their independence, social and occupational integration and participation in the life of the community. Article 26, according to its protection approach and structure, is similar to the aforementioned Article 25 on the social integration measures for the benefit of the elderly.

4.3.5. Solidarity

Probably the most controversial part of the Charter concerns the enshrinement of a series of economic and social guarantees in Chapter IV ("Solidarity"). The inclusion of fundamental social rights constitutes a contentious issue to this day with regard to the legal nature and scope of this right.[194]

In this connection, differentiation can be made between the Member States, whose constitutions guarantee social rights and take a positive view on the inclusion of such rights in the Charter of Fundamental Rights (such as, e.g., Germany, France, Italy, Spain and Portugal), on the one hand, and the Member States, which have not provided any fundamental social rights in their constitutions, and which rather confronted the integration of such rights in the Charter with reluctance (such as, e.g., the United Kingdom or Austria), on the other hand. The United Kingdom asserted especially persistent reservations against the expansion of legally binding social rights.[195]

---

193 Cf. Hans D. Jarass, EU-Grundrechte, ibid., p. 322.

194 Cf. Matthias H. Knecht, Die Charta der Grundrechte der Europäischen Union: Eine Würdigung der Entstehung und rechtsvergleichende grundrechtsdogmatische Analyse, 2005, p. 177 et seqq.; Michael Blank, Soziale Grundrechte in der Europäischen Grundrechtecharta, 2002; Jürgen Meyer/Markus Engels, Aufnahme von sozialen Grundrechten in die Europäische Grundrechtecharta?, in: ZRP 2000, p. 368.

195 Because of these reservations, the United Kingdom – together with Poland – ensured, in a protocol to the Lisbon Reform Treaty, an "opting out" clause for the application of the Charter. The Czech Republic is striving for accession to that protocol, see Point 5.3 below.

It can be asserted with good reasons that the extension of the Charter to social rights could probably be realised only because the Charter was not conferred any legally-binding force. Thus, the Convention of Fundamental Rights could, without any specific serious consequences, extensively follow the provisions of Europe's Social Charter and the Community Charter of Fundamental Social Rights of Workers.[196]

However, a waiver to include fundamental social rights in a comprehensive fundamental rights' catalogue of the Union could have sent negative signals at the international level. It could have been misunderstood as a backward step against the existing obligations of the EU Member States under international law, for instance, under the United Nations International Pact concerning economic, social and cultural rights (of 19.12.1966).

Moreover, the proponents of an integration of fundamental social rights aptly point out the interdependence and the interaction between the political and social rights. Since political rights could only be exercised with social guarantee, the fundamental social rights constitute their necessary supplementation; both the spheres could not be distinguished from each other without overlap.[197]

The title "Solidarity" (Chapter IV) comprises twelve articles (Article 27-38), which can be subdivided in four categories:[198]

- freedoms with social relevance, such as, e.g., the right of collective bargaining and action, including the right to strike (Article 28);
- fundamental economic and social rights, which justify claims for protection, such as, e.g., workers' right to information and consultation within the undertaking (Article 27), protection in the event of unjustified dismissal (Article 30), right to working conditions which respect health, safety and dignity (Article 31), prohibition of child labour and protection of young people at work (Article 32) or the right to legal, economic and social protection of the family, including the maternity protection at the place of work and the right to maternity leave (Article 33);

---

196 Cf. Dorothee von Arnim, Der Standort der EU-Grundrechtecharta in der Grundrechtsarchitektur Europas, ibid., p. 136; Klaus-Dieter Borchardt, in: Manfred A. Dauses (editor), Handbuch des EU-Wirtschaftsrechts, D. II. Sozialrecht, para 11 et seqq. On this point, see also: Jürgen Meyer/Markus Engels, ibid.

197 On this point, see: Günter Hirsch, in: Michael Blank, Soziale Grundrechte in der Europäischen Grundrechtecharta, 2002, p. 15.

198 Classification according to Christoph Grabenwarter, Die Charta der Grundrechte für die Europäische Union, ibid., p. 9 et seq. A tripartite classification (by omitting mere social principles, which enshrine no subjective rights) is done by Nina Philippi, Die Charta der Grundrechte der Europäischen Union, ibid., p. 30.

- fundamental economic and social rights, which justify the rights of participation, such as, e.g., the right of access to a free placement service (Article 29), the right of entitlement to social security benefits (Article 34), the right of access to preventive health care and the right to benefit from medical treatment (Article 35), as well as the right of access to services of general economic interest (Article 36);
- social principles, which do not justify any subjective rights, but only transfer the already existing Community objectives of the EC Treaty to the Charter of Fundamental Rights as horizontal provisions, thus, e.g., the health care (Article 35), the environmental protection (Article 37) and the consumer protection (Article 38).

Noteworthy is the fact that social guarantees in the strict sense, such as, for instance, the right to housing or the right to work, are not contained in the Charter. Article 34(3) only recognises the "right to social and housing assistance so as to ensure a decent existence for all those who lack sufficient resources". The mentioned assistance is governed by the Community law and national laws and practices. However, with the right to work, the Charter does not mean the right to a job; such a right would not be practically realisable[199] in an "open market economy with free competition"[200]

The most important of the individual fundamental rights guarantees under Chapter IV ("Solidarity") will be discussed below.

The workers' right to information and consultation within the undertaking (Article 27 of the Charter) has its origin in Europe's Social Charter and the Community Charter of Fundamental Social Rights of Workers (No. 17 and 18). According to the prevailing opinion, thereby, it is not a directly enforceable right, but, on the contrary, an objective, which will be concretised only in accordance with the implementing Community law and national laws and practices.[201] Therefore, one can rightly speak of a relative guarantee of fundamental rights.[202]

The right of collective bargaining and action enshrined in Article 28 of the Charter is modelled similarly as the aforementioned right to information and consultation; it is, to some extent, its legally logical continuation in the direction of a primary right to freedom of association (cf. Article 12(1) of the Charter, which,

199 Matthias Mahlmann, Die Grundrechtecharta der Europäischen Union, ibid., p. 435.
200 Cf. Article 119(1 and 2) TFEU (ex-Article 4(1 and 2) TEC).
201 Cf. Hans D. Jarass, EU-Grundrechte, ibid., p. 338; Eibe Riedel, in: Jürgen Meyer, Kommentar zur Charta der Grundrechte der Europäischen Union, 2003, p. 339.
202 Eibe Riedel, ibid., p. 346.

on its part, originates from Article 11 of the ECHR). The beneficiaries of this right are not only the individual employees and employers, but also their respective organisations. They are, in their capacity as the parties to a collective agreement – in accordance with the rules laid down by Community law and national laws and practices –, authorised to negotiate and conclude collective agreements at the appropriate levels and, in cases of conflict of interests, to take corrective actions to defend their interests, including strike actions. The counterpart of a lock-out as the means of industrial action of the employers' federations is not specifically mentioned in Article 28 of the Charter, however, should be affirmed in the perspective of the principle of equality of arms.

The access to a "free placement service" (Article 29 of the Charter) exhibits a close relationship with the freedom to choose an occupation and the right to engage in work (see above, Article 15 of the Charter). The free-of-charge aspect of the placement service represents a constitutional novelty. Since, however, from the mentioned provision, no obligation of the Member States or the Union arises to establish and to finance a placement service organised in any manner,[203] Article 29 restricts itself *de facto* to guarantee the non-discriminatory access to the existing placement services created by the State or with the assistance of the State.

Article 30 provides the protection in the event of unjustified dismissal, which can, however, be accorded only limited efficiency because this provision does not assure any objective level of protection, rather refers to the existing Community law and national laws and practices in this regard.

Article 31 of the Charter postulates in paragraph 1 a general right, which is vague to a large extent with regard to contents, to "working conditions which respect .... health, safety and dignity"; in paragraph 2, certain aspects of labour law have been concretised, for example, the employee's right to limitation of maximum working hours, to daily and weekly rest periods and to an annual period of paid leave. Although the European and national standards of protection have not been explicitly referred to, however, it's obvious that the applicable conventions and directives could be cited here as aids to interpretation.[204]

Article 32 on the prohibition of child labour and protection of young people at work enshrines special provisions for the protection of healthy, safe and dignified working conditions (within the meaning of Article 31). These latter provisions could, at the same time, be interpreted as *leges speciales* vis-à-vis the general provisions on the right to protection of children (Article 24, see above).

---

203 Cf. Sebastian Krebber, in: Christian Calliess/Matthias Ruffert, EUV/EGV. Das Verfassungsrecht der Europäischen Union mit Europäischer Grundrechtecharta, ibid., p. 2654.

204 Rudolf Streinz, EUV/EGV, Vertrag über die Europäische Union und Vertrag zur Gründung der Europäischen Gemeinschaft, 2003, p. 2628.

As supplementation to the general right to marry and right to found a family (Article 9), Article 33 of the Charter protects the institution of the family as an economic and social community. This Article should harmonise especially the family and professional life with each other, and should work towards flexibility in both these spheres of life. The maternity protection and the right to maternity leave under labour law are mentioned as specific protection objectives.

Articles 34, 35 and 36 have in common that they justify economic and social rights of participation, namely, the access to State or other public social security benefits and social assistance, access to health care and to services of general economic interest.

Article 34 of the Charter, which is unmistakably based, with regard to concept and structure, on Europe's Social Charter, that is to say, adopts its separation of social security and social assistance, guarantees a fundamental right to social equality with regard to entitlements to the social security benefits and social advantages in favour of everyone residing and moving legally within the European Union; the benefits and advantages are governed by the Community law and national laws and practices (Paragraphs 1, 2). In order to combat social exclusion and poverty, the Union recognises and respects the right to social and housing assistance so as to ensure a decent existence for those who need it. The Community law and national laws and practices have been referred to once again even in this respect (Paragraph 3). It is contentious as to what extent the addressed rights enshrine directly enforceable fundamental rights or just inchoate basic principles.[205]

In this context, it should be noted that although the constitutional traditions and the social legal systems of the Member States enshrine different rights with regard to the access to social benefits and their amounts, however, the right to minimum means of subsistence (minimex) is common to all the Member States.[206]

The right of everyone to benefit from medical treatment under the conditions established by national laws and practices is recognised within the scope of health care (Article 35, 1st Sentence). In addition, in the second sentence of this article – much like as already in Article 152(1) TEC (now: Article 168(1) TFEU) –, health care is recognised as a horizontal clause: "A high level of human health protection shall be ensured in the definition and implementation of all Union policies and activities".

Much like in the area of health care, the access to services of general economic interest is guaranteed as provided for in the rules laid down by national laws and

205 On this point, see: Hans D. Jarass, EU-Grundrechte, ibid., p. 362; Thorsten Kingreen, in: Christian Calliess/Matthias Ruffert, EUV/EGV, ibid., p. 2669.

206 Rudolf Streinz, EUV/EGV, ibid., p. 2631.

practices in accordance with the EC Treaty. This access shall promote the social and territorial cohesion of the Union (Article 36).

Reminiscent of some of the constitutions of the Member States, which recognise the environmental protection as a State objective, Article 37 enshrines a commitment to a high level of environmental protection and the improvement of the quality of the environment. These objectives must be integrated into the policies of the Union and ensured in accordance with the principle of sustainable development (horizontal clause).

Chapter IV ("Solidarity") concludes with a commitment to a high level of consumer protection as an integral part of the policies of the Union (horizontal clause, Article 38). A definition of the concept of consumer cannot be found in the Charter of Fundamental Rights. According to the understanding of consumer protection in Article 153 TEC (now: Articles 12 and 169 TFEU), however, the protection of the economic interests of the consumer should be in the foreground.[207]

4.3.6. Citizens' rights

The "citizens' rights" embodied in Chapter V of the Charter guarantee, first and foremost, rights to the citizens of the Union, as they have already been enshrined in the second part (Article 17-22) of the EC Treaty since the Maastricht Treaty. As one may expected, only the citizens of the Union shall be entitled to these fundamental rights, however, Chapter V also covers those citizens' rights, on which everyone can rely, consequently, even the nationals of third countries. To the latter rights belong, among others, freedom of movement and residence for the third country nationals (Article 45(2) of the Charter), furthermore, the universal, that this to say, applicable for all without distinction, "right to good administration" (Article 41 of the Charter), as well as its different forms of expression, such as the right of access to documents of the Community institutions (Article 42 of the Charter),[208] the right to refer to the "Ombudsman" (Article 43 of the Charter) and the right to petition the European Parliament (Article 44 of the Charter).[209] The three last-mentioned articles confer rights on the citizens of the Union, as well as

207 Cf. Johannes Christian Wichard, in: Christian Calliess/Matthias Ruffert, EUV/EGV, ibid., p. 2677 et seqq.

208 Article 42 exclusively refers to the documents of the European Parliament, Council and the Commission, not to any other acts of the administration with Community connection. This provision, therefore, does not justify a general right of access to the files on Community issues.

209 Already similar to Article 21 TEC in conjunction with Articles 194, 195 TEC (now: Article 24 TFEU in conjunction with Articles 227, 228 TFEU).

on any natural or legal person residing or having its registered office in a Member State.

However, in the stricter sense, the citizens' rights limit their scope of application to the citizens of the Union. They have the right to vote and to stand as a candidate at elections to the European Parliament in the Member State in which he or she resides (Article 39 of the Charter).[210] They further have the right to vote and to stand as a candidate at municipal elections in the Member State in which he or she resides (Article 40 of the Charter).[211]

Even the right to diplomatic and consular protection is laid out as a Union citizens' right: Every citizen of the Union shall, in the territory of a third country in which the Member State of which he or she is a national is not represented, be entitled to protection by the diplomatic or consular authorities of any Member State, on the same conditions as the nationals of that Member State (Article 46 of the Charter).[212]

Especially practical importance is ascribed to the "modern" everyone's right to a "good administration" (Article 41 of the Charter), which integrates several principles of administrative practice under the rule of law developed by the ECJ.[213] It aims to model the administrative acts of the Member States and of the Union efficiently and as closely as possible to the citizen.[214] Accordingly, every person has the right "to have his or her affairs handled impartially, fairly and within a

210 Already similar to Article 19(2) TEC (now: Article 22(2) TFEU).

211 Already similar to Article 19(1) TEC (now: Article 22(1) TFEU).

212 Already similar to Article 20 TEC (now: Article 23 TFEU).

213 It's still unsettled, whether Article 41 of the Charter also enshrines the procedural fundamental rights and the principle of the rule of law, praetorially developed and pronounced by the ECJ, such as the legality of administrative action, legal certainty or the protection of legitimate expectations, or whether the latter are superior maxims, which directly flow from the basic concept of justice. This question goes beyond whether the right to a "good administration" represents an – enforceable – individual right (so Georg J. Schmittmann, Rechte und Grundsätze in der Grundrechtecharta, 2007, p. 128; Hans D. Jarass, EU-Grundrechte, ibid., p. 399) or only an – indirectly enforceable – superior principle of law (so Jürgen Meyer/Markus Engels, Die Charta der Grundrechte der Europäischen Union, 2001, p. 31). Insofar apparent, the first judgement of the Court of First Instance of the European Communities (CFI) on Article 41 of the Charter was issued in 2002. Thereby, the CFI supportively referred to this provision so as to infer an obligation of the Commission for the impartial conduct in a formal review procedure: judgement of 4.4.2002, Glaswerke Ilmenau v Commission, Case T-198/01 R, EuGE 2002, II-2153, II-2184 et seq.

214 Cf. Matthias H. Knecht, Die Charta der Grundrechte der Europäischen Union: Eine Würdigung der Entstehung und rechtsvergleichende grundrechtsdogmatische Analyse, ibid., p. 199.

reasonable time by the institutions and bodies of the Union" (Article 41 (1)). This right includes, in particular (Article 41(2)):

– the right of every person to be heard, before any individual measure which would affect him or her adversely is taken;

– the right of every person to have access to his or her file, while respecting the legitimate interests of confidentiality and of professional and business secrecy;

– the obligation of the administration to give reasons for its decisions.

Moreover, from the right to a good administration, a right is derived for every person to have the Community make good any damage caused by its institutions or by its servants in the performance of their duties and, in fact, in accordance with the general principles common to the laws of the Member States (principle of Community liability, Article 41(3)).

Finally, the right to a good administration implies that every person may write to the institutions of the Union in one of the languages of the Treaties and must have an answer in the same language (Article 41(4)).

4.3.7. Justice

Under the title "Justice", Chapter VI of the Charter codifies constitutional procedural guarantees, which in essence correspond to the judicial procedural guarantees of the European Convention on Human Rights (in particular, its Articles 6, 7, 13).

Article 47 of the Charter is the central point, which, as "everyone's right", summarily lists the various forms of the right to efficient legal protection and a fair trial, which are traditionally recognised in all the constitutional States. In this connection, the case-law of the ECJ serves as an important starting point. In its judgement in the "Les Verts" case, it has qualified the European Economic Community as "a Community based on the rule of law, inasmuch as neither its Member States nor its institutions can avoid a review of the question whether the measures adopted by them are in conformity with the basic constitutional charter, the Treaty".[215]

Article 47 should be interpreted in the light of this case-law. Although it stipulates that effective remedies and fair trials (postulate of "*due process*" and "*fair trial*") must be available, however, does not give any specifications for the con-

215 Judgement of 23.4.1986, Les Verts v European Parliament, Case 294/83, ECR 1986, 1339, 1365 et seq.

crete embodiment of the system of legal protection and the types of procedures. In particular, this provision does not justify any right to a multi-stage procedure.[216]

More specifically, Article 47(1) guarantees everyone, whose rights and freedoms guaranteed by the law of the Union are violated, the right to an effective remedy before a tribunal. Article 47(2) grants everyone a right to a fair and public hearing within a reasonable time by an independent and impartial tribunal. The parties shall have the right to be advised, defended and represented before the court. Article 47(3) assures legal aid to the parties in need.

Additional fundamental guarantees related to criminal law and penal procedures are enshrined in Articles 48 to 50 of the Charter. They are partly based on the corresponding provisions of the ECHR, and partly on the law-making judicature of the ECJ.

Thus, Article 48(1) (analogous to Article 6(2) ECHR) guarantees the penal presumption of innocence in criminal law; Paragraph 2 of this article guarantees (analogous to Article 6(3) ECHR) the respect for the rights of defence of the accused, to which primarily belongs the right to a hearing. The classic prohibition of the retroactivity of criminal laws ("*nullum crimen, nulla poena sine lege*", analogous to Article 7 ECHR)[217], and the prohibition of the disproportionality of the penalty[218] are laid down in Article 49.

Finally, Article 50 of the Charter prohibits double penalty for the same criminal offence ("*ne bis in idem*", analogous to Article 4 of the Additional Protocol No. 7 to the ECHR).[219]

---

216 Cf. Udo Ostermann, Entwicklung und gegenwärtiger Stand der Europäischen Grundrechte nach der Rechtsprechung des Europäischen Gerichtshofs sowie des Gerichts erster Instanz, ibid., p. 215.

217 The principle of non-retroactivity of criminal laws is mitigated by the so-called "Radbruch's formula", whereupon the positive law has to yield to justice (natural law) in exceptional cases: Gustav Radbruch, Gesetzliches Unrecht und übergesetzliches Recht, in: Schweizerische Juristenzeitung (SJZ) 1946, p. 105; cf. Article 49(2) of the Charter.

218 The principle of proportionality between penalties and criminal offences (Article 49(3) of the Charter) is inferred in the literature from the human dignity in conjunction with the general personal rights and the rule-of-law principle, cf. Hans D. Jarass, EU-Grundrechte,ibid., p. 477.

219 For the case-law of the ECJ in this regard, see Point 3.6.8.5. above ("the ne bis in idem principle").

4.3.8. *General provisions*

Chapter VII of the Charter of Fundamental Rights enshrines general horizontal provisions on the effects of the Charter, especially concerning their "scope" (Article 51), the "scope of guaranteed rights" (Article 52), the "level of protection" (Article 53) and the "prohibition of abuse of rights" (Article 54).[220]

4.3.8.1. *Scope of the Charter of Fundamental Rights*

To determine the position of the Charter of Fundamental Rights within the fundamental rights architecture of the Union, first of all, the personal scope of application of the Charter should be focused upon. In this regard, Article 51(1) makes it clear that the Charter is addressed to the institutions and bodies of the Union with due regard for the principle of subsidiarity and to the Member States only when they are implementing Union law.[221]

The term "institutions and bodies of the union" used in Article 51(1) of the Charter should be understood in a non-technical sense, i.e., broadly. It refers to the European Council as the meeting of heads of State and/or government (as the only genuine institution of the Union, Article 4 TEU, replaced, in substance, by Article 15 TEU), as well as the institutions and bodies of the European Community (now: institutions and bodies of the European Union, Article 7 TEC, replaced, in substance, by Article 13 TEU).[222]

The Member States have been designated as the addressees of fundamental rights under the Charter only when they are implementing Union law.[223] The concept of implementation covers the administrative enforcement of primary or sec-

---

220 Article 51-54 of the Charter were fiercely debated in the Convention on Fundamental Rights till the very last minute. These provisions experienced substantial modifications in the final stage of elaboration. On this point, see: Holger Brecht, Änderungen an der EU-Grundrechtecharta. Korrekturen durch Verfassungskonvent und Regierungskonferenz sowie Konsequenzen für die Auslegung der Charta, in: ZEuS 2005, p. 363, 385 et seqq.

221 The term "addressed to" cannot be equated with "binding": provisions, which enshrine mere principles, although they are ascribed validity, however, have no direct binding effect for any addressees, see also Thorsten Kingreen, in: Christian Calliess/ Matthias Ruffert, EUV/EGV, ibid., p. 2707 et seqq.

222 Cf. Rudolf Streinz, EUV/EGV, ibid., p. 2651; Carolin Eisner, Die Schrankenregelung der Grundrechtecharta der Europäischen Union: Gefahr oder Fortschritt für den Grundrechtsschutz in Europa?, 2005, p. 88.

223 Cf. judgement of 13.4.2000, Karlsson, Case C-292/97, ECR 2000, I-2737, I-2760, para 37: "the requirements flowing from the protection of fundamental rights in the Community legal order are also binding on Member States when they implement Community rules".

ondary Community/Union law by the authorities of the Member States, on the one hand, however, on the other hand, also the enactment of national normative acts on the basis of Community/Union framework legislation, such as, e.g., the transposition of directives.[224]

It is questionable whether the criterion "when implementing Union law" mentioned in Article 51(1) of the Charter can be interpreted extensively beyond the wording in a manner that it should be considered to be fulfilled even when *in casu*, although the autonomous national law is applicable, it, however, pursues the objective to justify restrictions on the fundamental communitarian freedoms (market freedoms). The author of the present treatise affirms the questions posed because the contrarian, restrictive interpretation of Article 51(1) would deprive this provision of its *effet utile*.

If the scope of application of the Charter opens up *ratione personae*, it is incumbent upon the addressees of the fundamental rights to respect the rights enshrined in the Charter within the scope of their respective powers, to observe the principles and promote the application thereof (Article 51(1) 2nd sentence). The existing division of competences between the Union and the Member States remains explicitly unaffected by the Charter. *Ad abundantiam,* this is affirmed by the declaratory competence protection clause of Article 51(2), whereupon, the Charter does not establish any new power or task for the Community or the Union, or modify powers and tasks defined by the Treaties. Hereby, the apprehension, that the Union could gain in competences from the applicability of the communitarian fundamental rights, should be dispelled.[225]

From the aforesaid, it follows that the conflicts between the fundamental rights guarantees of the national constitutions and those of the Charter could appear only in the areas in which the actions of the Member States fall within the material scope of application of the Charter, that is to say, the Member States implement Union law (cf. Article 51(1) 1st sentence of the Charter). In these areas, there may be overlaps because the Member States are concurrently subject to two legal orders here, their own national laws and those of the Union in the form of the Charter of Fundamental Rights. Any conflicts should be solved according to the principle of maximum standards, i.e., that legal order should apply, which, in a specific case,

---

224 Cf. Josef Franz Lindner, Grundrechtsschutz gegen gemeinschaftsrechtliche Öffnungsklauseln – zugleich ein Beitrag zum Anwendungsbereich der EU-Grundrechte, in: EuZW 2007, p. 71, 72.

225 The cited provisions correspond to the case-law of the ECJ, whereupon, although respect for the fundamental rights is a condition for the legality of the Community acts, however, those rights cannot, in themselves, have the effect of extending the scope of the Treaty provisions beyond the competences of the Community: judgement of 17.2.1998, Grant/South-West Trains, Case C-249/96, ECR 1998, I-621, para 45.

guarantees the highest level of protection of fundamental rights. An amendment of the fundamental rights part of the national constitutions is not required as a precondition for the enactment of the Charter of Fundamental Rights because in areas in which the Member States (merely) apply the national law, they are exclusively subject to the commitment to national fundamental rights. The Charter does not supersede the national constitutions in areas, which apply to the respect for fundamental rights only at the national level.[226]

Although Article 51 of the Charter mentions the institutions and bodies of the Union, as well as the Member States, as the potential addressees of the fundamental rights, however, fails to mention a possible third-party effect (horizontal effect) of the fundamental rights in the Union. This circumstance could, as an *argumento e contrario,* be interpreted to the extent that individuals as the addressees of the fundamental rights generally and categorically segregate. But this interpretation cannot be followed in the light of the case-law of the ECJ. Rather, it is the established case-law of the Court of Justice that, under certain conditions, even individual persons could be bound by the fundamental guarantees. Primarily, this happens in cases of discriminations on grounds of nationality or in the area of gender equality.[227] Since the Charter is based on the basic principle of maximum legal protection (cf. Article 53), it appears to be desirable that the rights guaranteed by it do not lag behind the existing level of protection to which also belongs, as a matter of principle, the praetorially developed ability of the natural and legal persons to be addressees of the fundamental rights.

The Charter does not explicitly define who can be a beneficiary of the fundamental rights conferred by the Charter. Even in this respect, the case-law and the literature must be referred to: Expressed in simplified terms, it can be established that natural persons and legal persons governed by private law belong to the circle of potential beneficiaries of fundamental rights (rights-holders) within the meaning of the Charter. However, legal persons governed by public law, in particular, territorial subdivisions of the Member States, do not count among them.[228]

---

226 Cf. Commission of the European Communities, Communication from the Commission on the legal nature of the Charter of Fundamental Rights of the European Union, 11.10.2000, COM (2000) 644 final, p. 5. See also: Manfred Zuleeg, Zum Verhältnis nationaler und europäischer Grundrechte, Funktionen einer EU-Charta der Grundrechte, in: EuGRZ 2000, p. 511.

227 Carolin Eisner, ibid., p. 94. On this point, see also Point 3.4.1. ("Commitment to fundamental rights").

228 On the issue of the possession of fundamental rights, see: Matthias Mahlmann, Die Grundrechtecharta der Europäischen Union, in: ZEuS 2000, p. 419, 437; Nina Philippi, Die Charta der Grundrechte der Europäischen Union, 2002, p. 35. On this point, see also Point 3.4.2. (" Entitlement to fundamental rights").

4.3.8.2. Scope of guaranteed rights

Under the title "Scope of guaranteed rights", Article 52 specifies the conditions and the scope of possible restrictions on the rights and freedoms embodied in the Charter. This horizontal restrictive provision, which is highly significant in practice, sets out standard guidelines for the dogmatic structure of Union's fundamental rights. It is modelled closely on the structure of the doctrine of restrictions in the case-law of the ECJ:

Firstly, any limitation on the exercise of the rights and freedoms recognised by the Charter must be provided for by law and respect the essence (substance) of those rights and freedoms. Secondly, such limitations may be made only if they are necessary and genuinely meet objectives of general interest recognised by the Union or the need to protect the rights and freedoms of others. Finally, such limitations are subject to the principle of proportionality (Article 52(1)).

Article 52(1) of the Charter, thus, expresses constitutional principles, which are derived from the constitutional traditions of the Member States and also from the ECHR as the sources of the knowledge of law, and which have already found their way into the judicature of the ECJ.[229] This provision terms the restrictions on fundamental rights as the legal reservation ("Gesetzesvorbehalt") in formal respect and, in material respect, as the pursuit of a legitimate objective (requirements of the general interest or, alternatively, protection of competitive individual positions). The guarantee of the substance and the principle of proportionality are identified as the so-called limits of restrictions.[230] In this connection, especially the principle of proportionality should be highlighted, however, the ECJ does not restrict itself infrequently to the mere examination of the substance when analysing the fundamental rights.[231] It is also pointed out that several fundamental rights

---

229 Cf. Dororthee von Arnim, Der Standort der EU-Grundrechtecharta in der Grundrechtsarchitektur Europas, ibid., p. 317. It is noteworthy that the Charter of Fundamental Rights does not explicitly guarantee the so-called "absolute rights", i.e., rights, which are not subject to any kind of restrictions. However, the concept of "absolute rights" meets approval with Article 1 of the Charter, which declares "human dignity" to be "inviolable" (on this point, see Point 4.3.2. above). The same is applicable for the prohibition of torture and inhuman or degrading treatment or punishment, which, finally, are to be inferred from the human dignity (Article 4).

230 Definitions of the substance (essential content) and the proportionality cannot be found in the Charter of Fundamental Rights, so that for the clarification of these notions primarily the established case-law of the ECJ has to be referred to, which, on its part, is mainly based on the constitutional traditions of the Member States. On this point, see Points 3.5.3. and 3.6.7. above; cf. also Carolin Eisner, ibid., p. 141.

231 Cf. Markus Kenntner, Die Schrankenbestimmungen der EU-Grundrechtecharta – Grundrechte ohne Schutzwirkung?, in: ZRP 2000, p. 423, 424.

could be thoroughly subject to their own (vertical) restrictions or even a reservation under the national law and practices.[232] These specific restrictions, as *leges speciales,* take precedence in application over the general, horizontal restrictions.

Special provisions can be found in Article 52(2 and 3), which illuminate the relationship of the Charter of Fundamental Rights with the Community Treaties (or with the Treaty on European Union) and with the ECHR. These provisions adopt the fundamental rights recognised in the Treaties and the ECHR as Charter rights (so-called transfer clause). More specifically, the following should be noted:

- The rights recognised by the Community Treaties or the Treaty on European Union shall be exercised under the conditions and within the limits defined by those Treaties (Article 52(2)).
- In this context, a special practical relevance is ascribed to Article 52(3) of the Charter, which refers to the relationship of the Charter of Fundamental Rights with the ECHR. This relationship is characterised by the immanent risk of divergent lines of the case-law of the European Court of Justice (ECJ) and the European Court of Human Rights (ECtHR). In order to avoid, if possible, the conflicts between both the courts and the legal instruments formed by them, the rule is established that in case of corresponding rights in the Charter and the ECHR, these rights in both the texts shall have the same meaning and scope (conformity clause, Article 52(3) 1st sentence). The mentioned rule of interpretation, however, does not conflict with the right of the Union to grant more extensive protection (Article 52(3) 2nd sentence), thus, the ECHR only assures minimum standards.
- Article 52(3) of the Charter can be evaluated as the key standard for the determination of the position of the Charter in the existing system of protection of the European fundamental rights. Almost the entire substantive legal protection of the ECHR and its additional protocols has, thus, been incorporated into the Community/Union law, so that, irrespective of any formal accession, one can rightly speak of an already existing substantive accession of the Union to the ECHR. As a result, the case-law of the ECtHR is lastly relevant for the interpretation of the incorporated rights, which ensures that the endeavoured coherence of the European fundamental rights legal order can be retained.[233]

---

232 E.g., Articles 8, 9, 10(2), 14(3), 16, 17(1), 23, 27, 28, 30, 34, 35, 36 of the Charter.
233 Cf. Carolin Eisner, ibid., p. 150,; Dorothee von Arnim, ibid., p. 393.

4.3.8.3. Level of protection

Article 53 of the Charter enshrines another rule of interpretation. This stipulates, similar to Article 52(2 and 3), the relationship of the Charter of Fundamental Rights with the other fundamental rights' codifications, and in fact, within the meaning of a "most-favoured clause".[234] Unlike in the last-mentioned provisions, here, it's not about the influence of other fundamental rights guarantees for the interpretation and application of the Charter of Fundamental Rights, but, on the contrary, it concerns the consequences, which are to be drawn from the establishment of the Charter of Fundamental Rights for the interpretation and application of international and national fundamental rights regulations.[235]

Article 53 says that nothing in this Charter shall be interpreted as restricting or adversely affecting human rights and fundamental freedoms as recognised, in their respective fields of application, by Union law and international law and by international agreements of the Union, the Community or of all the Member States (including the ECHR), and by the Member States' constitutions.[236]

Thus, even Article 53 of the Charter is based on the basic assumption that this instrument, in no case, withdraws the level of protection of the existing – international or national – fundamental rights guarantees, but, on the contrary, should consolidate and develop the s*tatus quo* further on. From this perspective, Article 53 can be understood as a conflict-of-laws rule, which does not alter the applicable laws and the sources of the knowledge of law. It clarifies that a minimum standard should be stipulated only if similar fundamental rights, from different sources of the law, are applicable to a specific situation, and the person concerned relies on the law that is most favourable to him or her.[237]

4.3.8.4. Prohibition of abuse of rights

The final provision of the Charter (Article 54) can be understood as the charter-specific expression of the general prohibition of abuse. It protects the existence of fundamental rights under the Union law from abusive utilisation. Accordingly,

---

234 Hans-Werner Rengeling/Peter Szczekalla, Grundrechte in der Europäischen Union – Charta der Grundrechte und allgemeine Rechtsgrundsätze, 2004, p. 267.

235 Thorsten Kingreen, in: Christian Calliess/Matthias Ruffert, EUV/EGV, ibid., p. 2739.

236 Article 53 of the Charter of Fundamental Rights is broadly based on the identical Article 53 of the ECHR, whereupon, this Convention "is not to be interpreted in a manner which shall be construed as limiting or derogating from any of the human rights and fundamental freedoms which may be ensured under the laws of any High Contracting Party or under any other agreement to which it is a party".

237 Dorothee von Arnim, ibid., p. 369.

it prohibits interpreting anything in this Charter as implying any right to engage in any activity or to perform any act aimed at the destruction of any of the rights and freedoms recognised in this Charter or at their limitation to a greater extent than is provided for herein.

Article 54, which, according to objectives and wording, is based on Article 17 of the ECHR[238], meets the concerns of the "democracy capable of defending itself";[239] it should protect the elementary rights and freedoms from erosion. As a result, the protection against the abuse of law should be reached for, if the rights of private persons or sovereign authorities are used to restrict or to misuse the rights of others in a disproportionate manner. In such a case, a reliance on those fundamental rights, which were specifically abused, should be ruled out.[240]

4.4. Summary appraisal of the Charter of Fundamental Rights

To summarise the above, it can be noted as an achievement of the Charter of Fundamental Rights that it has consolidated this totality of rights, which were dispersed over a plurality of national and international instruments, in a single document; it enshrines the key substance of the European *acquis* in the area of the fundamental rights.

Thus, the Charter, as a comprehensive document, enshrines all the relevant personal (civil, political, economic and social) rights, including the rights arising from the citizenship of the Union, and, therewith, emphasises the principle of indivisibility of fundamental rights. The classic international law distinction between the civil and political rights, on the one hand, and the economic and social rights, on the other hand, was abolished. Rather, the Charter grouped all the rights round a few fundamental principles, such as the human dignity, the elementary freedoms, equality, solidarity, citizenship of the Union and justice. With the exception of the rights, which are specially linked to the citizenship of the Union (e.g., participation in the elections to the European Parliament or to the local elections), the Charter enshrines "everyone's rights", which are characterised by that they benefit everybody, irrespective of the nationality or the domicile.

---

238 Article 17 ECHR says: "Nothing in this Convention may be interpreted as implying for any State, group or person any right to engage in any activity or perform any act aimed at the destruction of any of the rights and freedoms set forth herein or at their limitation to a greater extent than is provided for in the Convention".

239 Rudolf Streinz, EUV/EGV, ibid., p. 2657.

240 Hans-Werner Rengeling/Peter Szczekalla, Grundrechte in der Europäischen Union, ibid., p. 272.

Another credit to the Charter of Fundamental Rights exists in the acknowledgement of a certain number of "modern" rights, which round off and supplement the "classic" rights, as they have been enshrined in the European Convention on Human Rights. New rights of such a kind cover, for example, the data protection or the rights in the area of bioethics, which should meet the challenges of the modern information technology or the genetics respectively. Another type of so-called modern rights results from the need for administrative transparency; it relates, among others, to the access to documents of the Community/Union institutions.

It must also be pointed out that the rights enshrined in the Charter not only provide extensive instruments for the protection of the individuals, but also contain objective principles to control the political and social order. In this dual perspective, they represent a significant source of inspiration and orientation, above all, for the case-law of the ECJ.[241] They fulfil their dual function as guarantees of individual protection and as objective ordo-political criteria primarily with regard to the institutions and bodies of the Union, but also in relation to the Member States, be it in the administrative implementation of Union law or in the adoption of measures to restrict individual rights, for instance, on grounds of *ordre public*. In this connection, the rights recognised by the Charter often assume the function of restrictive provisions vis-à-vis the interventions in the individual legal positions.[242]

Finally, it should not go unrecognised that the Charter of Fundamental Rights promotes and strengthens the consensus among the Member States and the citizens of the European Union and strengthens the common identity thereby. This document makes it clear that the Union and its Member States are committed to common democratic-constitutional ideals and convictions, which are characterised by the predominance of law. Within this meaning, democracy is understood not only as a formal form of government, but also as a community of political, spiritual and moral values, which is substantially expressed in the fundamental rights.

---

241 Cf. Commission of the European Communities, Communication from the Commission on the legal nature of the Charter of Fundamental Rights of the European Union, 11.10.2000, COM (2000) 644 final, p. 5 et seq.

242 Cf. Manfred A. Dauses, The Protection of Fundamental Rights in the Community Legal Order, in: ELR 1985, p. 398, 418.

5. On the path to a legally binding catalogue of fundamental rights

5.1. Preliminary remark

The European Charter of Fundamental Rights, which was solemnly proclaimed at the summit of Nice on 7.12.2000, originally had – as depicted above – the character of a non-binding proclamation, which was to be imputed to the *soft law*.

Non-binding catalogues of fundamental rights already entail as such certain unmistakable advantages: they impart transparency and clearness, and are closer to the citizens and, thus, fulfil a beneficial leading and guiding role. On the other hand, a purely praetorian, unwritten system of protection of the fundamental rights shows fundamental weaknesses: the elements of protection, the circle of beneficiaries of fundamental rights and the entities bound by the fundamental rights, the restrictions on fundamental rights and the limits of restrictions are, in the absence of the transparency of purely casuistic decisions, not revealed to the laymen, not even to the expert just like that. It rather requires an intensive analysis of individual judgements, and perhaps also of the relevant technical literature, in order to get an adequate overview of the development and the status of protection of the fundamental rights in the Union. This amount of work and understanding although cannot be cut down entirely, but can at least be reduced considerably by a systematic and concise codification even of non-binding nature. In general, codifications have the advantage of being linguistically compact and concise; mostly, they abstain from legal dogmatic technical terms and constructions, which are incomprehensible to the laymen, as a result of which the critical content can be made more sensible.[243]

Another advantage of a, even if non-binding, codification of the fundamental rights exists in reflecting a consensus on the common convictions and moral values, which visibly demonstrates the transition from an economic to a legal community[244] and, in addition, strengthens the integration.

243 Gunter M. Hoffmann, Grundrechte in Europa – braucht Europa einen Grundrechtskatalog?, 1995, p. 67 et seq., with references.

244 Siegbert Alber/Ulrich Widmaier, Die EU-Charta der Grundrechte und ihre Auswirkungen auf die Rechtsprechung. Zu den Beziehungen zwischen EuGH und EGMR, in: EuGRZ 2000, p. 497, 499.

But since no direct political or social capacity to make policy emanates from mere proclamations, they could only guarantee limited legal certainty and legitimation. The complete realisation of these objectives can only be achieved by legally binding documents, whereupon, however, it is to be pointed out more precisely that even the content of written fundamental rights is finally characterised and formed by the case-law.

Accordingly, a demand has been raised for decades in the European law literature for a written, binding catalogue of fundamental rights.[245] The Convention of Fundamental Rights, under the chairmanship of the former German President Roman Herzog, also proceeded on the assumption of this postulate, which has not lost its actuality ever since. Accordingly, the Charter should be implemented in two stages: the first step of a solemn proclamation should be followed by the second step of consideration as to how the adopted Charter should be integrated into the primary law of the Union. Thereby, a "Constitution for Europe", which was in preparation at that time, was thought of first and foremost. Already during the elaboration of the Charter, the finality of its integration into the future constitution should be kept in view; consequently, the Charter should be shaped "as though" it would definitely become an integral part of the "Treaty establishing a Constitution for Europe". This so-called "as though" approach was confirmed by the European Council at its meeting in Cologne on 3 and 4 June 1999 and, thereafter, by the European Parliament.[246]

Vice versa the "Treaty establishing a Constitution for Europe", the ratification of which, as is well-known, failed because of the negative outcome of the plebiscites in France and the Netherlands, envisaged that the Charter of Fundamental Rights should be included in the Constitution as Chapter II. Therewith, the Charter should not remain a mere solemn proclamation with sheer symbolism of words

245 On this point, see Udo Ostermann, Entwicklung und gegenwärtiger Stand der europäischen Grundrechte nach der Rechtsprechung des Europäischen Gerichtshofs sowie des Gerichts erster Instanz, ibid., p. 220 et seq., with references; Ingolf Pernice, Gemeinschaftsverfassung und Grundrechtsschutz – Grundlagen, Bestand, Perspektiven, in: NJW 1990, p. 2409, 2418 et seq.; Meinhard Hilf, Ein Grundrechtskatalog für die Europäische Gemeinschaft, in: EuR 1991, p. 19 et seqq.; Manfred A. Dauses, Der Schutz der Grundrechte in der Europäischen Gemeinschaft, in: JÖR 1982, p. 1, 17 et seqq.; Ellen Chwolik-Lanfermann, Braucht die Europäische Union einen Grundrechtskatalog?, in: ZRP 1995, p. 126, 129 et seq.

246 Conclusions of the Presidency of the Cologne European Council, 3 and 4 June 1999, Annex IV. Resolution A5-0064/2000 of the European Parliament on the elaboration of a Charter of Fundamental Rights of the European Union: Minutes of the plenary session of 16 March 2000; Resolution B5-767/2000 of the European Parliament on the Charter of Fundamental Rights: Minutes of the plenary session of 3 October 2000.

and sheer theoretical value as a source of the knowledge of law, but should attain a direct legally binding force at the highest rank in the hierarchy.

Even after the failure of the pretentious constitutional plans, the endeavour to elevate the Charter of Fundamental Rights to the rank of primary law was not given up. Rather, a consensus was achieved in the European Council that the Charter should now be structurally linked to the – considered as functional successor to the Treaty establishing a Constitution for Europe – Lisbon "Reform Treaty". This latter Treaty did not choose the technical solution of an incorporation of the Charter of Fundamental Rights into the corpus of the Treaty, which was, although signed by all the Member States, however, mainly due to the negative referendum in Ireland, was not immediately ratified by all the Member States. Rather, one was contented with a mere cross-reference to the Charter of Fundamental Rights, combined with the note that the referred document shall have the same ranking as the Treaties:

"The Union recognises the rights, freedoms and principles set out in the Charter of Fundamental Rights of the European Union of 7 December 2000, as adapted at Strasbourg, on 12 December 2007, which shall have the same legal value as the Treaties" (Article 6(1) 1st sentence of the EU Treaty in the version of the Treaty of Lisbon).

The following statements, first of all, look into an analysis of the arguments, which speak in favour of a legally-binding force of the Charter of Fundamental Rights (Point 5.2.). Thereafter, the technical modalities for vesting the Charter of Fundamental Rights with legally-binding force will be discussed (Point 5.3.). Subsequent to that, those arguments will be discussed, which are in favour or against an accession of the Union to the ECHR (Point 5.4.), and the modalities for an accession of the Union to the ECHR will be analysed (Point 5.5.).

5.2. Arguments in favour of a legally-binding force of the Charter of Fundamental Rights

A deliberative legal analysis shows a vast majority of arguments in favour of a transformation of the Charter of Fundamental Rights from a non-binding proclamation to a fundamental element of the binding primary law of the Union. The most important argument in favour of such a step is the legal certainty, i.e., the predictability, calculability and reliability of the Union's legal protection,[247] thus,

247 Gunter M. Hoffmann, ibid., p. 12; Rudolf Streinz, Bundesverfassungsgerichtlicher Grundrechtsschutz und Europäisches Gemeinschaftsrecht, 1989, p. 425; Christoph Sasse, Der Schutz der Grundrechte in den Europäischen Gemeinschaften und seine

elements, which could not be adequately guaranteed by the *soft law*, even in conjunction with a stabilising case-law of the ECJ.[248] On the other hand, the possible disadvantage of a crystallisation of the law, which accompanies the statics of the codified texts, is likely to be marginal already due to the strong influence of a flexible judicature of the ECJ.

The demand for a binding catalogue of fundamental rights is also closely connected with the problem of the lack of legitimacy and democratic deficit of the Union. The central point of the discussion in this regard is the petitum of a strengthening of the democratic legitimacy of the Union by increasing the competences of the European Parliament. This theory assumes that a Union-specific catalogue of fundamental rights should not be enacted without the important cooperation of the European Parliament as the democratically elected representation of the European peoples. If this catalogue not only stipulates the rights and freedoms, which have already been elaborated praetorially, but also develops them further, and creates new rights over and above that, thus, the cooperation of the European Parliament strengthens the position of the beneficiaries of fundamental rights and creates additional democratic legitimacy.

Although another, extenuating theory likewise applies to the lack of legitimacy and democratic deficit of the Union, however, connects it to the currently restricted progress of integration of the Union. From this perspective, a binding catalogue of fundamental rights could indeed improve the democratic-constitutional functions already in the current state of integration, but would still not be indispensable for the time being. A binding catalogue of fundamental rights is, namely, a traditionally integral part of the State constitution and, therewith, a key element of the statehood. Therefore, a Union's own, binding catalogue would be indispensable only if the Union gets ready to take the still outstanding quantum leap from being

---

Lücken, in: Hermann Mosler/Rudolf Bernhardt/Meinhard Hilf, Grundrechtsschutz in Europa, 1977, p. 51 et seqq.; Dieter Feger, Die Normsetzung auf dem Gebiet der Grundrechte in den Europäischen Gemeinschaften – Der Europäische Gerichtshof (EuGH) als Rechtsetzungsorgan, in: DÖV 1987, p. 322 et seqq.

248 Differentiations can be made between the relative legal certainty, on the one hand, which arises from an autonomous, coherent catalogue with clear and precise rules, and the absolute legal certainty, on the other hand, which flows from the legally-binding force of such a catalogue, and results in that the authorities and courts must apply the catalogue as the applicable law. It's quite obvious that an absolute obligation to apply the law can only relate to a legally-binding Charter, which the authorities and courts must apply already due to its legally-binding force, and on which the rights-holders can rely, i.e., on the basis of which they can secure the certainty on the application of the law. On this point, see the general reflections Gunter M. Hoffmann, ibid., p. 13 et seqq.

a federation of states to a federal State, vested with the so-called "jurisdiction over jurisdiction [Kompetenz-Kompetenz]".[249]

The author of the present study inclines towards the opinion that the necessity to vest the European Charter of Fundamental Rights with legally-binding force already flows, in the current legal status, from the postulate of legal certainty and the principle of legitimation and democracy. The theory, according to which a binding catalogue of fundamental rights at the Union-level would be imperatively required only if the Union mutates from a federation of states into a federal State, is herewith rejected. It may hardly be conceivable that a European Federal State will emerge out of states, which have a binding catalogue of fundamental rights as an integral part of their constitutions – and such a binding catalogue of fundamental rights is the significant attribute of their statehood -, unless the Union, as the predecessor of a possible European Federal State, already has such catalogue.

5.3. Modalities for vesting the Charter of Fundamental Rights with legally-binding force

As demonstrated above, it was thought, first of all, to incorporate the Charter of Fundamental Rights into the planned "Treaty establishing a Constitution for Europe". Even after the ambitious plans of a constitutional process failed and, therefore, a new starting point came into being with regard to the future shape of Europe, the key objective to integrate the Charter of Fundamental Rights with binding effect into the primary law of the Union was maintained without any change. In this connection, the general opinion in political, as well as in legal circles, optimistically trusted that, although the efforts for a European constitution have shattered for a foreseeable future, however, the substituting Lisbon Reform Treaty, even if with certain amendments and supplementations, will become *lex lata*.

Against this factual background, it seems appropriate to discuss and evaluate several possible options for an integration of the Charter of Fundamental Rights into the Union Treaty law from the doctrinal point of view:[250]

- An integration of the Charter of Fundamental Rights directly into the *corpus* of the Union Treaties would be the closest and most intensive form of connection. Therewith, the Charter would be the central, integral part of the Treaty into which it is integrated. Should, as envisaged in the Lisbon Treaty, a reor-

249 Cf. Gunter M. Hoffmann, ibid., p. 85 et seqq., 100 et seqq., 108et seq.
250 On this point, see: Jörg-Philipp Terhechte, Verfassung ohne Rhetorik – Zur neuen Gestalt der Europäischen Union, in: EuZW 2007, p. 521.

ganisation of the existing Treaties into a Union Treaty, as a Basic Treaty, and a secondary Treaty on the Functioning of the Union be contemplated, in view of the high significance of the Charter, its incorporation into the Basic Treaty would seem desirable.

- The integration of the Charter of Fundamental Rights in the Treaties, especially in the Basic Treaty, in the form of an annexed protocol (analogous to Article 311 TEC), would substantively make the Charter an integral part of the Treaty concerned, and would, consequently, accord it the same legal position as that Treaty. But this solution would have certain disadvantages in symbolic sense. It could create the impression that the provisions under the Charter are a matter of minor importance, which, therefore, are referred to a subordinated rank from the technical point of view.
- The weakest form of integration of the Charter in the Union law exists in a mere reference to the Charter in the Treaties. This approach quite clearly has an even lower symbolic value than the option of an annexed protocol. Since by the cross-reference as such, no automatic statement is made on the hierarchical rank and the legal effects of the referred legal provisions, it is appropriate to elucidate these issues by corresponding determinations in the reference texts. In the Lisbon Treaty, this has been appropriately done in a manner that explicitly the equal ranking of the Charter and the Treaties is postulated (Article 6(1) 1st sentence TEU in the version of the Lisbon Treaty, see above Point 5.1.).
- A wording, according to which the Charter would have to be looked upon as a mere source of the knowledge of general fundamental principles of law, consequently, only as a secondary source of law, would be of little help. In such a case, the Charter would lack the direct legally-binding force.

In this connection, particular attention deserves the question whether it would be consistent with the legally-binding force of the Charter to exclude individual Member States from the obligation to observe the fundamental rights guaranteed in the Charter, that is to say, to abandon the principle of unity of Community law with regard to a certain group of addressees of the fundamental rights. This question is gaining importance in the light of the view represented by the Republic of Poland and the United Kingdom. Both States want to accept a legally binding force of the Charter only insofar as it does not imply the ability of the European Court of Justice or any court or tribunal of Poland or of the United Kingdom to find that the laws or practices of these Member States are inconsistent with the fundamental rights, freedoms and principles enunciated in the Charter.[251]

251 Cf. Protocol (No. 30) on the application of the Charter of Fundamental Rights of the European Union to Poland and the United Kingdom, annexed to the Lisbon Treaty.

A similar "opting-out" clause is intended to apply for the Czech Republic. This Member State has not obtained a derogation in a special protocol annexed to the Lisbon Treaty. It has, however, during the process of ratification, expressed the petitum to be granted an exemption. As a result, the European Council adopted a declaration to the effect that on the occasion of the next amendment to the Treaties, i.e., in connection with the admission of new Member States, the Czech Republic will be allowed to accede to the special Polish-British protocol.[252] The adoption of a separate protocol for the Czech Republic, however, was denied.

Although the petitum of a "multi-speed Europe" meets with considerable political reservations, however, this concept is not without precedent, one only thinks of the exceptional rules for individual Member States in the area of European Monetary Union or the "opting out" of the United Kingdom from the obligations of the Social Policy Protocol (No. 14), on the basis of which the "Social Policy Agreement" was agreed upon between the Member States, with the exception of the United Kingdom.[253] Seen from a legal dogmatic point of view, consequently, the derogatory way described here would not be objectionable, even though it may seem less desirable in terms of legal policy.

5.4. Arguments in favour of an accession of the Union to the ECHR

In political, just as in legal circles, a strong tendency exists in favour of an accession of the Union to the European Convention on Human Rights.[254] Such a step

---

252 As the amendments to the Union Treaties do not have a retroactive effect, the treaties apply for the Czech Republic, during the period between the entry into force of the Lisbon Treaty (1.12.2009) and the entry into force of a possible derogatory protocol, in their original version. It means that, for the time being, the Czech Republic is fully bound by the rights, freedoms and principles set out in the Charter of Fundamental Rights, without being in a position to invoke a special exemption. Only with the entry into force of a relevant amendment, a possible exemption will become effective.

253 The Protocol (No. 14) on social policy was adopted as an annexed protocol to the Maastricht Treaty on European Union of 7.2.1992, with the approval of the United Kingdom, however, excluding the obligations arising from the Protocol for this Member State. With the coming into force of the Amsterdam Treaty of 2.10.1997, the provisions of the Protocol were – without the exceptional rule for the United Kingdom – incorporated into the amended EC Treaty.

254 An accession is postulated with certain regularity in the literature: e.g., Ingolf Pernice, Gemeinschaftsverfassung und Grundrechtsschutz – Grundlagen, Bestand, Perspektiven, ibid., p. 2418; different opinion by Manfred A. Dauses, Der Schutz der Grundrechte in der Europäischen Gemeinschaft, ibid., p. 19 et seqq. In a Memorandum of 4.4.1979, the European Commission formally suggested this step for the first time: Bulletin of the European Communities, supplement 2/79; on this point, see:

could, if necessary, be taken parallel to a declaration of the legally-binding force of the Charter of Fundamental Rights. Therewith, the Convention, which is presently cited only as a source of the knowledge of law to find the general principles of Union law, would be transformed into a directly effective, binding instrument of Union law.

The petitum of an accession of the Union to the ECHR is based implicitly on the general provisions of the European Charter of Fundamental Rights (see above, Point 4.3.8.), on the one hand; on the other hand, Article 6(2) TEU, in the version of the Lisbon Treaty, explicitly commits to such an accession.[255] The new provision makes it clear, at the same time, that the existence and the scope of the competences of the Union laid down in the Treaties shall not be affected by such an accession:

> "The Union shall accede to the European Convention for the Protection of Human Rights and Fundamental Freedoms. Such accession shall not affect the Union's competences as defined in the Treaties" (Article 6(2) TEU, new version).

As already indicated, the enactment of an autonomous binding Charter of Fundamental Rights, and the accession of the Union to the European Convention on Human Rights are two mutually independent ways of realising an effective monitoring of compliance with the fundamental rights in the Union. An accession to the ECHR could, therefore, be envisaged not only in place of an integration of the Charter in the Union Treaties, but also besides this. However, in case of the enactment of a binding Union's catalogue, the additional step of an accession to the ECHR seems practical only if it entails an additional gain in legal clarity, legal certainty and legal protection.

The ECHR enshrines an autonomous catalogue of fundamental rights, which codifies and systemises the common European constitutional values of the Member States of the Council of Europe, to which all the EU Member States belong. It has, however, *ratione materiae,* a narrower scope of application than the Charter of Fundamental Rights because its main focus is on protecting the classic civil and

---

Roland Bieber, Bemerkungen zum Memorandum der Kommission betreffend den Beitritt der EG zur Konvention über den Schutz der Menschenrechte und Grundfreiheiten, in: EuGRZ 1979, p. 338 et seqq.; Dietmar Nickel, Zum Grundrechtsdefizit der Europäischen Gemeinschaften, in: ZRP 1980, p. 161, 164 et seqq.; Heribert Golsong, Nochmals: zur Frage des Beitritts der Europäischen Gemeinschaften zur Europäischen Menschenrechtskonvention, in: EuGRZ 1979, p. 70.

255 The Draft Treaty establishing a Constitution for Europe (Article I-7(2) of the Thessaloniki Draft) had already broached the issue of the accession of the Union to the ECHR by granting the Union the entitlement to accession. However, this provision was cancelled thereafter in the final text of the Constitutional Treaty.

political rights, however, only a basic set of economic rights. On the other hand, the Charter of Fundamental Rights, according to the scope of responsibilities and duties of the Union, comprehensively guarantees economic rights and freedoms as well. A legal deficit of the ECHR, moreover, exists in that it was concluded as an "old" Convention, already in 1950, thus, in the immediate post-war period, and does not contain any so-called "modern" rights, whose need for protection has become evident only in recent times.

Therewith, the legal protection benefits resulting from an accession of the Union to the ECHR are rather likely to be marginal from an objective perspective. However, such an accession, in any case, promises a benefit from an institutional perspective: an accession would fit the Union in a Europe-wide system of monitoring the fundamental rights. The advantage of such an external monitoring and controlling is unmistakable, if one bears in mind that the case-law of the ECJ shows a strong tendency to administer justice in an "integration-friendly" manner, i.e., when balancing the values and interests between the individual rights and the interests of the Union, to attach particular importance to the latter.

In this context, it should be remembered that, although all the EU Member States are contracting parties to the ECHR, the institutional system of legal protection established by the Convention, in particular, the interstate complaint (Article 33) and the individual complaint (Article 34), cannot be relied upon against the acts of the authorities of the Community and/or the Union, so long as the Community and/or the Union, on its part, is not a contracting party to the Convention formally.[256]

Irrespective of the aforementioned considerations, it should not be overlooked that an accession of the Union to the ECHR would be, in any case, attached a high symbolic value, which consists in making visible to the outside world the allocation of the Union to the common European values of human rights, the rule of law and democracy.

5.5. Modalities for an accession of the Union to the ECHR

A formal accession of the Union to the ECHR would presuppose legislative adjustments on the part of the Convention, as well as on the part of the Union:

256 Cf. Decision of the European Commission of Human Rights of 10.7.1978, Application N° 8030/77, Confédération Française Démocratique du Travail v European Communities, on this point, see Point 3.2.2.3 above.

- On the part of the Convention, the formal barrier that the ECHR is conceived as an agreement between States must be removed, i.e., only States, and in fact, members of the Council of Europe may belong and/or accede to it as signatories (Article 59(1)). But this barrier can easily be removed by a corresponding amendment of the mentioned final provision of the ECHR, thus, by a saving clause in the form that the accession would be open to even international and supranational organisations with specific competences, or that the European Community and/or the European Union would specifically be mentioned as contracting parties.
- Should the Community and/or the Union be incorporated in the group of contracting parties to the ECHR, grave consequences would arise from it for the integration of the Community/Union jurisdiction in the institutional structure of the Convention. In such a case, namely, the EC/EU would be equated with a State, which would mean that even the clause of exhaustion of domestic remedies, before the European Court of Human Rights deals with a case ("*local remedies rule*", Article 35(1)), would analogously apply to the exhaustion of legal remedies provided in the Community/Union legal order. In practical significance, in view of the compliance with the fundamental rights protected by the ECHR, this results in subordinating the European Court of Justice (ECJ) to the European Court of Human Rights (ECtHR). As a result, delicate problems relating to the delimitation of competences could arise because the ECJ has the jurisdiction in the last instance for monitoring the compliance with the fundamental rights guaranteed by the Union law.[257]
- Even on the part of the Union, an accession of the Union to the ECHR, under the mentioned circumstances, would entail significant legal effects. The accompanying institutional adjustments of the current Union system would be of constitutional significance and, therefore, could be effected only by an amendment to the Treaty.[258] The general empowering clause ("*implied powers clause*") of Article 352 TFEU would be insufficient as the legal basis.

257 In this connection, the ECJ warned in its Opinion of 28.3.1996 of an accession of the Community to the ECHR. Such a system of external fundamental rights monitoring "would result in an essential change in the present Community system for protecting human rights, as [it] would entail the Community's integration into a different institutional system governed by international law and the incorporation of all the provisions of the Convention into Community law." This quotation makes it clear that the ECJ primarily fears the overshadowing by – and being placed under – external, international power structures, Opinion 2/94 of 28.3.1996, ECR 1996, I-1759, I-1789.

258 Cf. the aforementioned Opinion 2/94, ibid. It is emphasised in it once again that an accession of the EC to the ECHR would change the basic judicial structure of the Community because therewith the ECtHR would be the court adjudicating at last instance, in place of the ECJ, for the interpretation and application of the ECHR-fun-

6. Institutional protection of fundamental rights

6.1. Basic principles of the system of legal protection in the Community/Union

A concluding chapter is dedicated to the system of legal protection in the Community and the Union, and its suitability for an efficient legal protection of fundamental rights guaranteed by the Community and/or the Union.

The provisions concerning the protection of fundamental rights in the Community/Union, in particular, the European Charter of Fundamental Rights, do not enshrine any special provisions on the judicial protection in legal relationships in which the fundamental rights guaranteed by the Community/Union are involved. The system of legal protection in the Community/Union will be summarily described below, and it will be examined with regard to the question whether it fulfils the requirements of efficiency and completeness in its current form or whether it must be developed further. Within this scope, above all, it should be analysed whether, for instance, the necessary developments could be brought about by adjusting the existing ways of action and forms of judgement or whether the creation of new legal institutions, especially a specific fundamental rights complaint, is needed.

6.1.1 The European Community as a Community based on law

The European Community, which was transformed into the European Union with the signing of the Maastricht Treaty on 7.2.1992, is more than just an association for special economic purposes and a concept of political order. It is also shaped as a Community based on law, which pursues its widespread integration objectives within the scope of an autonomous, directly applicable legal order which takes

---

damental-rights in the Community legal order as well. But such a profound change could be effected only by a substantial amendment of the communitarian provisions for legal protection, consequently, an amendment of the primary law.

precedence. The term "Community based on law" was coined by the ECJ, apparently based on the German concept of the rule of law ("Rechtsstaat").[259]

In the light of the case-law of the ECJ, the "rule of law" of the Community/Union manifests itself especially in the formal primary fundamental right to effective remedy[260] for all the legal relationships substantiated by the Community and/or Union law. The requirement for legal protection, in particular, shows three factors:

- Binding acts of the Member States and the institutions of the Community and/or the Union are subject to the review of the legality of acts in the light of the Community/Union law, which has primacy, whereupon the fundamental rights play a prominent role:

  > "The European Economic Community is a Community based on the rule of law, inasmuch as neither its Member States nor its institutions can avoid a review of the question whether the measures adopted by them are in conformity with the basic constitutional charter, the Treaty".[261]

- The subjective rights conferred by the Community or Union legal order must be enforceable in an efficient judicial procedure.[262] This is applicable, in particular, vis-à-vis the violations of the rights by the public authorities, and in fact, both by the Community or Union institutions and by the Member States.[263]
- Under certain preconditions, the requirement for legal protection under Community or Union law can even include the obligation to grant temporary legal protection.[264]

---

259 Judgement of 23.4.1986, Les Verts v European Parliament, Case 294/83, ECR 1986, 1339, 1365 et seq.

260 On this point, see: Christian Calliess, Kohärenz und Konvergenz beim europäischen Individualschutz. Der Zugang zum Gericht im Lichte des Grundrechts auf effektiven Rechtsschutz, in: NJW 2002, p. 3577.

261 Judgement of 23.4.1986, ibid.

262 Judgement of 12.3.1987, Commission v Germany, "purity law for beer", Case 178/84, ECR 1987, 1227, 1274.

263 Judgement of 15.5.1986, Johnston, Case 222/84, ECR 1986, 1651, 1682; judgement of 15.10.1987, Heylens, Case 222/86, ECR 1987, 4097, 4117.

264 Judgement of 19.6.1990, Factortame, Case C-213/89, ECR 1990, I-2433.

6.1.2. Dualistic structure of Community/Union jurisdiction

Litigations concerning Community or Union law can be carried out both before the institutional Union courts and the national courts. The mutual delimitation of competences is governed by the principle of the conferral of competences ("compétence d' attribution"), according to which the institutional Union courts may act only within the limits of the powers conferred upon them by the Union law (Article 5(1) TEU; cf. ex-Article 5(1) TEC; ex-Article 3(1) Euratom Treaty). In this respect, their jurisdiction is mandatory and exclusive; a parallel jurisdiction of the national courts is excluded. However, if the competences have not been conferred on the institutional Union courts, the Union's litigations fall under the exclusive jurisdiction of the national courts.[265] Consequently, those are the Union judges of the *ius commune*.

Therefore, the Union's system of legal protection has a dual structure. The jurisdiction is divided between the Union courts in the institutional sense (Court of Justice of the European Union = ECJ, General Court of the European Union = GC and the subordinated specialised courts, e.g., the European Civil Service Tribunal), which centrally ensure the unity and uniform application of the Union law, and the courts of the EU Member States, which have to – within the scope of their jurisdictions conferred on them by the national law and according to the organisational and procedural law of the national courts – interpret and apply the Union law, and in doing so, they could, for the clarification of the questions of Union law, which are relevant for the decision, request the ECJ to give "legal assistance" in a preliminary ruling procedure (Article 267 TFEU; ex-Article 234 TEC; ex-Article 150 Euratom Treaty). In their capacity as the Union courts in the functional sense, they have to – just as the ECJ, GC and the subordinated specialised courts – guarantee the full effectiveness of the relevant European law and, in particular, to protect the rights, which it confers upon the individuals.[266]

The statements below are restricted to the description of the Union's jurisdiction in the institutional sense, i.e., the proceedings before the ECJ, the GC and the subordinated specialised courts, as far as these proceedings could be relevant for protection of fundamental rights in the Union.

265 Cf. Article 274 TFEU, ex-Article 240 TEC, ex-Article 155 Euratom Treaty, whereupon disputes to which the Union is a party shall not on that ground be excluded from the jurisdiction of the courts or tribunals of the Member States, save where jurisdiction is conferred on the Court of Justice by the Treaties.

266 Thus, e.g., judgement of 9.3.1978, Simmenthal, Case 106/77, ECR 1978, 629, 643 et seq.

6.1.3. Roles and responsibilities of the institutional Union courts

The Union Treaties describe the role of the ECJ, the GC and the specialised courts, which share the Union's judicial powers[267], comprehensively in the words: "The Court of Justice of the European Union .... shall ensure that in the interpretation and application of the Treaties the law is observed" (Article 19(1) TEU; cf. ex-Article 220(1) TEC; ex-Article 136(1) Euratom Treaty). This phrase is incomplete inasmuch as the "observance of the law", which is incumbent upon the mentioned Union courts, does not confine itself to the interpretation and application of the primary Union law, but also covers the examination of the validity, interpretation and application of the secondary law, as well as the finding and determination of the content of the general principles of the Union law. In addition, it contains only a general description of tasks, whereas the jurisdictions of the ECJ, the GC and the subordinated specialised courts, according to the principle of the conferral of competences ("*compétence d'attribution*"), arise from the specific provisions on jurisdiction laid down in the Union Treaties, as well as in the Statute and the Rules of Procedure of the courts:

- The general preconditions for a referral to the ECJ/GC (and to the subordinated specialised courts), as well as the various types of procedures are enshrined in Articles 258-280 TFEU (ex-Articles 226-244 TEC; ex-Articles 141-159 Euratom Treaty).
- These provisions of the Treaties are supplemented by the Statute of the Court of Justice, which is laid down in a separate protocol[268], which, on its part, defines the scope for the Rules of Procedure of the ECJ, GC and the European Civil Service Tribunal.

267 Specialised courts were originally mentioned as "judicial panels" (Article 220(2) TEC; Article 136(2) Euratom Treaty), but were renamed under the Lisbon Treaty (Article 19(1) TEU).

268 Protocol on the Statute of the Court of Justice: this Protocol also contains a Title (Title IV) on the Court of First Instance and an annex on the European Civil Service Tribunal: Protocol No. 6 on the Statute of the Court of Justice, imprinted in annex "C. Protocols annexed to the Treaty on European Union, to the Treaty establishing the European Community and to the Treaty establishing the European Atomic Energy Community", consolidated version of the Treaty on European Union and the Treaty establishing the European Community (Treaty of Nice), OJ. 2006, C 321 E, 203. Therewith, the Treaty of Nice has a single statute, which unites the three statutes EEC/EC, ECSC, Euratom existing till that time, whereupon it is to be noted that the ECSC Treaty had already lapsed on 23.7.2002, before the Treaty of Nice came into force.

- The procedural law in the strict sense (course of proceedings, hearing of evidence, summoning, service of process, time-limits, jurisdiction of the plenum and chambers, legal effect, enforcement, requests for legal assistance, legal aid, criminal complaint for a violation of oath among the many), as well as the details of the constitutions of the courts can be found in the Rules of Procedure enacted by the ECJ or the GC with the approval of the Council.[269]

With regard to the substantive division of jurisdiction between the ECJ and the GC, which was established as Court of First Instance (CFI) in 1988[270], it is to be mentioned that the latter – after successive expansions of its jurisdiction – today decides all the direct actions at first instance, with the exception of specific proceedings classified as "constitutional", among which, in particular, the actions brought by a Member State count. The latter procedures are reserved for the ECJ in the first and last instance, just as the requests for preliminary rulings and applications for the delivery of opinions on the external relations of the Communities (Article 256(1.1) TFEU; ex-Article 225(1.1) TEC; ex-Article 140 a(1.1) Euratom Treaty in conjunction with Article 51 of the Statute of the Court of Justice). Insofar the GC has jurisdiction at the first instance, an appeal (French: "*pourvoi*"), limited to questions of law, can be brought against its decisions before the ECJ (Article 256(1.2) TFEU; ex-Article 225(1.2) TEC; ex-Article 140 a(1.2) Euratom Treaty in conjunction with Articles 56-61 of the Statute of the Court of Justice, Articles 110-123 Rules of Procedure of the ECJ).

269 The Rules of Procedure of the Court of Justice of the European Communities of 19.6.1991, OJ. L 176 of 4.7.1991, p. 7, last amended by the Council Decision of 15.1.2008, OJ. L 24 of 29.1.2008, p. 9. Supplementary Rules of Procedure of the Court of Justice of the European Communities of 4.12.1974, OJ. L 350/29, last amended on 21.2.2006, OJ. 2006, L 72/1. Rules of Procedure of the Court of First Instance of the European Communities of 2.5.1991, OJ. 1991, L 136/1, last amended on 12.6.2008, OJ. 2008, L 179/12. Rules of Procedure of the European Union Civil Service Tribunal, OJ. 2007, L 255/1.

270 So as to reduce the workload on the ECJ and to improve the legal protection of the individuals, the CFI was assigned to the ECJ (Council Decision 88/591/ECSC, EEC, Euratom of 24.10.1988, OJ. 1988, L 319/1; corrigendum in: OJ. 1989, L 214/4; consolidated version of the amended Decision in: OJ. 1989, C 215/1). Amending Council Decision 93/350/ECSC, EEC, Euratom of 8.6.1993, OJ. 1993, L 144/21; amending Council Decision 94/149/ECSC, EC, Euratom of 7.3.1994, OJ. 1994, L 66/29. With the Maastricht Treaty on European Union of 7.2.1992, the establishment of the CFI was guaranteed directly in the primary law (Article 225 TEC; Article 140a Euratom Treaty). These legal bases were subsequently expanded by the Amsterdam Treaty of 2.10.1997 and, thereafter, once again by the Treaty of Nice of 26.2.2001 and the Lisbon Treaty of 13.12.2007.

Specialised courts could be attached to the GC for specific matters. An appeal – basically limited to questions of law – is admissible against their decisions before the GC (Articles 19 TEU, 257 TFEU; ex-Articles 220(2), 225a TEC; ex-Articles 136(2), 140b Euratom Treaty). At present, on this legal basis, a European Civil Service Tribunal exists, which has jurisdiction at the first instance in disputes between the Communities and their servants, and an appeal (also on matters of fact) against its decisions can be brought before the GC.[271]

6.1.4. Procedural law

In the further course of this study, several types of procedures before the ECJ/GC will be described, with special focus on their significance with regard to the judicial protection of fundamental rights. The analysis is based on the usual categorisation of the procedures in litigious procedures (direct actions) and preliminary ruling procedures. The third category of procedures, the procedure to obtain an opinion concerning the compatibility of an envisaged international agreement of the Community or the Union with the Treaties (Article 218(11) TFEU; ex-Article 300(6) TEC) will not be addressed. The latter procedure is purely an interinstitutional instrument, which does not exhibit any close relationship with the protection of individual rights.

6.1.4.1. Litigious procedure

The litigious (contradictory) procedures are characterised by that a plaintiff, who asserts a claim relying upon the Community law, and a defendant, who, as a rule, contests this claim, are pitted against each other (so-called direct actions). The most relevant types are the Treaty infringement procedure, the actions for annulment and for failure to act and the action for damages.

6.1.4.1.1. Treaty infringement procedure

6.1.4.1.1.1. Presentation of the case

In the Treaty infringement procedure (Articles 258-260 TFEU; ex-Articles 226-228 TEC; ex-Articles 141-143 Euratom Treaty), the ECJ decides, in the first and last

---

271 Cf. Annex to the Protocol on the Statute of the Court of Justice, in particular, Articles 1 and 9 of this annex.

instance, on the actions brought by the European Commission[272] or a Member State, which seek a declaration that a (another) Member State has failed to fulfil an obligation under the Union Treaties. Infringements of the Treaties are equated with infringements of the secondary Community or Union law, which is based on the Treaties, as well as infringements of the – unwritten – general principles of Community or Union law, under which fall primarily the fundamental rights protected in the European Union. In this context, the dogmatic question may be permitted, whether an infringement of the fundamental rights, which are applicable as general principles of Union law, should not be automatically qualified as an infringement of Article 6(3) TEU and, therewith, as a direct, and not just an indirect infringement of the Treaty.

The judicial stage of the Treaty infringement procedure is preceded by administrative preliminary proceedings, which aim to achieve the legal clarification of the contentious behaviour of the State, and the proper realisation of which is a precondition for the admissibility of the action to be examined by the court. In the preliminary proceedings, the defendant State should be given the opportunity to submit its observations. If it indicates that it will not follow the legal opinion of the Commission, the Commission issues a reasoned opinion ("*avis motivé*") declaring that it has failed to fulfil its obligations as alleged, and fixes a time-limit to remedy the infringement. After an unsuccessful expiry of the time-limit, the Commission or the interested Member State can bring an action before the ECJ (Article 258(2) TFEU, Article 259(2-4) TFEU; ex-Article 226(2), ex-Article 227(2-4) TEC; ex-Article 141(2), ex-Article 142(2-4) Euratom Treaty). Bringing a court action is not bound to any procedural time-limits. It is a non-justiciable discretionary decision; a right of the individual to initiate a Treaty infringement procedure does not exist.[273]

In the event the action is admissible and well founded, the ECJ declares that the defendant Member State has failed to fulfil an obligation under the Treaties. Thereby, it is irrelevant, which State authority or body is responsible for the incriminating infringement of the Union law, and even if it's an independent institution[274] (parliament, court, central national bank) by virtue of constitution or law. Rather, according to the general principles of international law, the Member States must accept full liability for the acts and omissions of their national sovereign

---

272 See in this regard: Claus-Dieter Ehlermann, Die Verfolgung von Vertragsverletzungen durch die Kommission – Europäische Gerichtsbarkeit und nationale Verfassungsgerichtsbarkeit, in: Festschrift für Hans Kutscher, 1981, p. 135.

273 Judgement of 1.3.1966, Lütticke, Case 48/65, ECR 1966, 27; judgement of 14.2.1989, Star Fruit, Case 247/87, ECR 1989, 291; Decision of 30.3.1990, Emrich, Case C-371/89, ECR 1990, I-1555.

274 Judgement of 18.11.1970, Commission v Italy, Case 8/70, ECR 1970, 961.

authorities at all institutional levels (federal, provincial and municipal levels, and the miscellaneous public authorities and institutions).[275] The determination of an infringement presupposes only the existence of an objectively unjustified violation of the Treaties, a misconduct is not required. According to the established case-law, a Member State may not plead provisions, practices or circumstances existing in its internal legal system in order to justify a failure to comply with the obligations incumbent upon it under Community/Union law.[276]

The final judgment on the merits is a declaratory judgement. By its very nature, it is not enforceable, rather the unsuccessful Member State shall, on its own responsibility "be required to take the necessary measures to comply with the judgment of the Court" (Article 260(1) TFEU; ex-Article 228(1) TEC; ex-Article 143(1) Euratom Treaty). In doing so, it has a political discretion, if several options exist to remedy the infringement established.

Non-compliance with this obligation to observe the law can, on its part, constitute a subject-matter of another Treaty infringement procedure, whereby, since the Maastricht Treaty on European Union, on application of the Commission, payment of a lump sum fine or a penalty can be imposed by a second court ruling (Article 260(2,3) TFEU; ex-Article 228(2, 3) TEC; ex-Article 143(2, 3) Euratom Treaty).[277]

---

275 Judgements of 2.2.1982, Commission v Belgium, Joined Cases 71/81 and 73/81, ECR 1982, 175 or 189. The conduct of the public bodies of the Member States should be attributed to the Member State, even if the central authority has no means, for instance, to urge the defaulting regions to fulfil the obligations: judgement of 14.1.1988, Commission v Belgium, Joined Cases 227-230/85, ECR 1988, 1, 11.

276 Judgements of 2.2.1982, Commission v Belgium, Joined Cases 71/81 and 73/81, ibid.; judgement of 28.3.1985, Commission v Belgium, Case 215/83, ECR 1985, 1039, 1054; judgement of 24.7.1988, Commission v Italy, Case 225/86, ECR 1988, 2271, 2279.

277 The Lisbon Reform Treaty has expanded the scope of the mentioned provisions in a manner that the mere omission by the Member State concerned to communicate the measures for implementing a directive can already lead to the imposition of a lump sum amount or penalty payment. For reasons of transparency, the Commission had notified, first of all, in two Communications of the years 1996 and 1997, the criteria, which it intends to follow when such penalties are applied for. The Communications of 1996 and 1997 were to be superseded by a Communication of 12.12.2005 on the method of calculating the penalty payments provided for pursuant to Article 228 TEC, SEC (2005) 1658. Thereby, the penalty is given precedence over the lump sum amount. The penalty is calculated on the basis of day fines. Such a calculation arises from a multiplication of a standard flat-rate amount (Euro 600 per day) by a coefficient for seriousness and a coefficient for duration. This result is again multiplied by a country factor, taking into account the capacity of the Member State to pay and the number of votes it has in the Council. In addition, a lump sum amount can be imposed, the method of calculation of which largely coincides with the method for

6.1.4.1.1.2. Assessment of the case with regard to the protection of fundamental rights

The Treaty infringement procedure is an important instrument to ensure the compliance with the Union law by the Member States. It exhibits the aspects of an action brought by an institution and also those of legal supervision proceedings. Basically, it is also suitable as an instrument to monitor the respect of the fundamental rights, which are protected under the Union law, by the Member States. The circumstance that the judgment upholding the complaint is a non-enforceable declaratory judgment, which is based on the obligation of the Member States to observe the law, does not conflict with its efficiency, the more so as the non-compliance with the obligation to observe the law can constitute the subject-matter of another Treaty infringement procedure in which pecuniary sanctions could be imposed upon the Member State in default.

The efficiency with regard to the protection of fundamental rights under the Treaty infringement procedure is, however, challenged by that this procedure, in its present form, is not accorded any direct function to protect the individuals. Although individuals could complain to the Commission or a Member State, and thus suggest initiation of proceedings, however, they do not have any enforceable right to initiate and conduct such a procedure; an indictment enforcement procedure ["Klageerzwingungsverfahren"] is not provided.[278] Even less could natural or legal persons, even if their own (fundamental) rights have been infringed, bring a Treaty infringement procedure before the ECJ. The procedure is rather understood as an instrument for legal supervision, and the right of action in this regard is dogmatically derived from the function of the Commission and the Member States as the "guardians of the Treaties" and as guardians of lawfulness in the Community/Union. Such a task has not been assigned to the individual person according to the fundamental structure of the Union's legal order.

---

the calculation of the penalty amount. In the judgement of 4.7.2000, Commission v Greece, Case C-387/97, the ECJ had ordered, for the first time, a Member State to pay a penalty (Euro 20,000 per day of delay), ECR 2000, I-5047.

278 Judgement of 1.3.1966, Lütticke, ibid.; judgement of 14.2.1989, Star Fruit, ibid.; Decision of 30.3.1990, Emrich, ibid.

6.1.4.1.2. Actions for annulment and for failure to act[279]

6.1.4.1.2.1. Presentation of the cases (Generalities)

In contrast to the Treaty infringement procedure that is directed against a Member State's conduct, which is contrary to the Union Law, the actions for annulment and for failure to act are directed against an action or omission by the Community/ Union institutions.

By the action for annulment (Articles 263, 264 TFEU; ex-Articles 230, 231 TEC; ex-Articles 146, 147 Euratom Treaty), the annulment of the legislative acts (legal acts adopted jointly by the European Parlament and the Council by legislative procedure, Article 289 TFEU), the legally-binding acts of the Council, of the Commission and of the European Central Bank, as well as the acts of the European Parliament, of the European Council and of the bodies, offices or agencies of the Union intended the produce legal effects vis-à-vis third parties can be sought. Actions for annulment against the recommendations and opinions, which are non-binding according to the typology of the Union legal acts (cf. Article 288(5) TFEU; ex-Article 249(5) TEU; ex-Article 161(5) Euratom Treaty), are explicitly excluded. These are to be equated with other, "atypical" expressions of opinion or intention by the Union institutions, which do not have legally-binding force, and which, therefore, could not substantiate any obligations for the individuals or impose burdens in some other way; in this respect, an interest in bringing an action for annulment does not exist.[280]

---

279 See in this regard: Hans-Wolfram Daig, Nichtigkeits- und Untätigkeitsklagen im Recht der Europäischen Gemeinschaften – unter besonderer Berücksichtigung der Rechtsprechung des Gerichtshofs der Europäischen Gemeinschaften und der Schlussanträge der Generalanwälte, 1985. In this connection, the proceedings in which the Court has unlimited jurisdiction with regard to penalties ("*recours de pleine juridiction*") are not dealt with. The relevant provisions (Article 261 TFEU; ex-Article 229 TEC; ex-Article 144 Euratom Treaty) do not justify legal action on their own, rather only expand the jurisdiction of the Community Courts arising from Articles 263, 264 TFEU (ex-Articles 230, 231 TEC; ex-Articles 146, 147 Euratom Treaty, action for annulment) by empowering the latter not only to annul, but also to amend certain specific sanctions applied by the European Parliament and/or the Council. These procedures, the practical significance of which is given, above all, in Community antitrust actions, do not show any specific links to the legal actions on infringements of fundamental rights.

280 These include, e.g., action programmes, such as the "general programmes" envisaged in Article 54(1) (old version), 63(1) (old version) TEC for the abolition of restrictions on freedom of establishment and freedom to provide services, which enshrine political objectives only. The same applies to the decisions or the declarations of the Council – and, a fortiori, of the European Council – with predominantly political content

The action for annulment is modelled on the "*recours pour excès de pouvoir*" (ultra vires) of the French administrative law; it resembles the action for annulment before the administrative courts under the German law, but also takes over certain functions of the action for the issue of an administrative act (if the action for failure to act is not relevant in such a case). Its objective is to monitor the legality of administrative acts; in addition, it ensures the judicial protection of individuals.

The action for annulment is supplemented by the action for failure to act (Article 265 TFEU; ex-Article 232 TEC; ex-Article 148 Euratom Treaty) by which a declaration can be sought that the European Parliament, the Council, the Commission or the European Central Bank has infringed the Treaty by "failing to act" (omission to take a decision). Consequently, in the system of legal protection established by the Treaties, the action for failure to act supplements the action for annulment in case the unlawful conduct consists in a failure to act on the part of the Community institution concerned or the European Central Bank.

6.1.4.1.2.2. Specificities of the action for annulment

The relevant provisions (Article 263, 264 TFEU; ex-Articles 230, 231 TEC; ex-Articles 146, 147 Euratom Treaty), in their version applicable before the Maastricht Treaty on European Union came into effect, enshrined only the review of the legality of the acts of the Council and the Commission. The widening of the potential circle of defendants to the European Parliament and the European Central Bank by the Union Treaty codifies the recent case-law of the ECJ concerning the European Parliament's passive capacity to be a party to legal proceedings[281], on

(e.g., concerning the questions of principle relating to economic and monetary union). However, the international agreements of the Communities with third countries or international organisations (which, from the Community's point of view, are acts of the Council as the contracting body, cf. Article 218 TFEU; ex-Article 300 TEC) are voidable with the action for annulment. According to the established case-law, they form an "integral part of the Community legal order": e.g., the judgement of 30.4.1974, Haegemann, Case 181/73, ECR 1974, 449, 460; judgement of 26.10.1982, Kupferberg, Case 104/81, ECR 1982, 3641, 3662. The power assigned to the ECJ by Article 218(11) TFEU (ex-Article 300(6) TEC) for delivering an opinion on the compatibility of a such a planned agreement, i.e., which is still being prepared, with the Union Treaties does not exclude the *a-posteriori*-supervision of the agreements in force. Admittedly, any annulment by the ECJ would be considerable only for the Community side (and, if need be, the EU Member States), not for the opposite side (third countries or international organisations). Actions for annulment against international agreements of the Communities have not been brought until now.

281 Judgement of 23.4.1986, Les Verts v European Parliament, Case 294/83, ECR 1986, 1339.

the one hand, and takes into consideration the assignment of acting powers to the European Central Bank, on the other hand (cf. Article 132 TFEU; ex- Article 110 TEC). The European Council's passive capacity was added by the Lisbon Treaty.

According to the current legal position, first of all, the Member States, the European Parliament, the Council and the Commission are entitled to bring an action, thereafter, the Court of Auditors, the European Central Bank, the Committee of the Regions and, finally, "any natural or legal person" (Article 263(2-4) TFEU; ex-Article 230(2-4) TEC; ex-Article 146(2-4) Euratom Treaty). Even with regard to the active capacity to be a party to legal proceedings, the successive adjustments to the Treaties have codified the institutional developments and the case-law of the ECJ[282].

Subject to certain exceptions, the ECJ has the jurisdiction, at the first and last instance, for the actions for annulment by the Member States, Union institutions and bodies or the European Central Bank. The actions for annulment of other plaintiffs should be brought before the GC at the first instance, against whose decisions an appeal, limited to the questions of law, can be lodged with the ECJ (Article 256(2) TFEU; ex-Article 225(2) TEC; ex-Article 140a(2) Euratom Treaty in conjunction with Article 51(1, 2) of the Statute of the Court of Justice).

As to the interest in bringing an action/need of legal protection: The Member States, the European Parliament, the Council and the Commission need not prove any special interest in bringing an action ("privileged applicants"), Article 263(2) TFEU; ex-Article 230(2) TEC; ex-Article 146(2) Euratom Treaty. However, the Court of Auditors, the European Central Bank and the Committee of the Regions are permitted only to bring actions for annulment "for the purpose of protecting their prerogatives" ("partially privileged applicants"), Article 263(3) TFEU; ex-Article 230(3) TEC; ex-Article 146(3) Euratom Treaty, i.e., in particular, for safeguarding their own institutional position.

However, natural or legal persons ("non-privileged applicants") may only "institute proceedings against an act addressed to that person or which is of direct and individual concern to them, and against a regulatory act which is of direct concern to them and does not entail implementing measures" (Article 263(4) TFEU). Among the non-privileged individual applicants count also the organisational public bodies of the Member States, if they have their own legal personality, thus, for instance, autonomous local authorities or a national central bank.

---

282 In its judgement of 22.5.1990 (European Parliament v Council, "Chernobyl", Case C-70/88, ECR 1990, I-2041, I-2072), the ECJ had, for the first time, – contrary to its earlier case-law – conferred on the European Parliament the right to bring an action for annulment, provided that the action seeks only to safeguard the Parliament's prerogatives and is founded only on submissions alleging their infringement.

The cited provision, which was introduced by the Lisbon Reform Treaty, replaces the following previous text: "Any natural or legal person may institute proceedings against a decision addressed to that person or against a decision which, although in the form of a regulation or a decision addressed to another person, is of direct and individual concern to the former" (ex-Article 230(4) TEC; ex-Article 146(4) Euratom Treaty).

A comparison of both texts suggests that, apart from minor linguistic modifications, they have two alternative criteria of admissibility in common, namely (a) the requirement that the action is directed against an act which is addressed to the plaintiff, and (b) the requirement that the challenged act is of direct and individual concern to the plaintiff. Among the latter category of challengeable acts also count the aforementioned acts which are addressed to the plaintiff, as a sub-category. The Lisbon Treaty has added as third alternative criterion (c) the requirement that the action is directed against a "regulatory act" which is of direct, but not necessarily of individual concern to the plaintiff, on condition, however, that this regulatory act does not entail implementing measures.

In practice and in the light of the jurisprudence of the European Court of Justice, the plaintiff's lack of *individual concern* is the main obstacle for the admissibility of an action for annulment brought by a natural or legal person against a normative act of the Union. According to established case-law of the ECJ, a non-privileged plaintiff may be individually concerned by a legally-binding normative act (in particular, a regulation) or by a decision directed at another – also a Member State – only if the legal act concerned "affects him by reason of certain attributes which are peculiar to him or by reason of circumstances in which he is differentiated from all other persons and by virtue of those factors distinguished individually as in the case of the person addressed".[283] This is not the case, if the measure in question has a "general application"[284] and its elements are objectively defined, thus the plaintiff is concerned only because of its affiliation to a "category of persons regarded generally and in the abstract"[285] and, in fact, even if "the

283 Judgement of 15.7.1963, Plaumann, Case 25/62, ECR 1963, 211, 238.

284 Judgement of 6.10.1982, Alusuisse, Case 307/81, ECR 1982, 3463, 3472.

285 As regards decisions: judgement of 5.5.1977, Koninklijke Scholten Honig, Case 101/76, ECR 1977, 797, 807; judgement of 10.6.1982, William and Bethell, Case 246/81, ECR 1982, 2277, 2291; judgement of 14.7.1983, Spijker Kwasten, Case 231/82, ECR 1983, 2559, 2566; judgement of 17.1.1985, Piraiki-Patraiki, Case 11/82, ECR 1985, 207, 243; judgement of 2.2.1988, von der Kooy, Joined Cases 67,68 and 70/85, ECR 1988, 219, 267; judgement of 14.2.1989, Lefebvre, Case 206/87, ECR 1989, 275, 288; As regards regulations: judgement of 1.4.1965, Sgorlata, Case 40/64, ECR 1965, 295, 311; judgement of 18.11.1975, CAM, Case 100/74, ECR 1975, 1393, 1404; judgement of 3.5.1978, Töpfer, Case 112/77, ECR 1978, 1019, 1030; judgement of 26.4.1988, Asteris and Greece v Commission, Joined Cases 97, 193, 199

number or even the identity of the persons to whom a measure applies can be determined more or less precisely, as long as it is established that the measure is applied by virtue of an objective legal or factual situation defined by the measure in question in relation to its purpose" (so-called "Plaumann" formula).[286]

In light of the cited "Plaumann" formula, as a rule, an individual concern of the citizens or undertakings by a normative act (regulation, directive etc.) seems to be excluded. The hurdles for proving the individual concern are so high that a right of natural or legal persons to bring legal proceedings can be assumed only in rare individual cases. Even the *ratio decidendi* of the recent, differentiating line of case-law, of not leaving the individuals without the protection of the law if, due to the specificities of the case, their subjective rights are severely infringed by normative law,[287] may hardly be applied in case of measures with uniform general normative content.

The CFI (now: GC) has recently followed a new course to deal more leniently with the precondition of the admissibility of the individual concern. According to this approach, an individual concern is already assumed if a regulation affects the legal position of a person "in a manner which is both definite and immediate, by restricting his rights or by imposing obligations on him".[288]

This argument of the lower court, which was apparently aimed at widening the protection of individual rights, was, however, overruled by the ECJ in the appeals procedure: According to the system for judicial review of the legality, which was established by the Treaty, a natural or legal person could bring an action challenging a regulation only if it is concerned both directly and individually. Although this last condition must be interpreted in the light of the principle of effective judicial protection by taking account of the various circumstances that may distinguish a plaintiff individually, such an interpretation cannot have the effect of setting aside the condition in question, expressly laid down in the Treaty, without going beyond the jurisdiction conferred by the Treaty on the Community Courts.[289]

In the light of this reluctant attitude of the ECJ with regard to the criterion of individual concern, the new provision of Article 263(4) TFEU and, in particular,

---

and 215/86, ECR 1988, 2181, 2205; Decision of 20.5.1987, Champlor, Joined Cases 223-235/86, ECR 1987, 2251, 2255.

286 Judgement of 15.7.1963, Plaumann, ibid., 238 et seq.

287 E.g., the judgement of 16.5.1991, Extramet Industrie, Case C-358/89, ECR 1991, I-2501, para 13; judgement of 18.5.1994, Codorniu, Case C-309/89, ECR 1994, I-1853, para 19.

288 Judgement of 3.5.2002, Jégo-Quéré v Commission, Case T-177/01, EuGE 2002, II-2365 II-2383.

289 Judgement of 25.7.2002, Unión de Pequeños Agricultores v Council, Case C-50/00 P, ECR 2002, I-6677, I-6735 et seq.; judgement of 1.4.2004, Jégo-Quéré v Commission, Case C-263/02 P, ECR 2004, I-3443, I-3457 et seq.

the new conditions of admissibility for proceedings against directly applicable "regulatory acts" deserve special attention. Because of the traditionally rigid interpretation of the requirement of individual concern for the actions of annulment of natural and legal persons, Article 263(4) TFEU is intended to fill, at least partially, the gap in the system of legal remedies, which has emerged for the natural and legal persons, by omitting the admissibility criterion of individual concern under specific conditions.

A critical analysis, however, suggests that, although Article 263(4) TFEU, third alternative, undoubtedly assumes a useful gap-filling function, it will probably fail to ensure a comprehensive and effective system of judicial protection of individual rights. Two reasons lead to that conclusion:

- First, the term "regulatory act" is not directly defined in the Lisbon Treaty, however, semantic clues can be found in the likewise amended Paragraph 1 of Article 263 TFEU. This new provision replaces the words "acts adopted jointly by the European Parliament and the Council" (i.e., legal acts, which were adopted under the codecision procedure) by "legislative acts". It follows from this that the "regulatory acts" are legal instruments on the level of the hierarchy of norms below the "legislative acts", which were not adopted jointly in the codecision procedure by the Parliament and the Council. Thereby, these are "simple" regulations of the Council or derivative regulations of the Commission enacted on the basis of a Council regulation (tertiary regulation), which do not require any implementing measures and, consequently, could not be challenged incidentally by means of such a measure. "Legislative acts", however, are not covered by the cited Treaty provision. Consequently, proceedings could not be instituted by natural or legal persons against "legislative acts" which are not of direct *and* individual concern.
- Secondly, an action for annulment could not be brought by natural or legal persons against a "regulatory act" which entails implementing measures. This rule applies irrespective of whether the implementing measures at issue themselves could be challenged by the plaintiff. In other words, annulment proceedings brought by natural or legal persons against regulatory acts could be declared inadmissible, because of the mere existence of implementing measures , even if there is no remedy against the implementing measures themselves, i. e., those measures could not be challenged by the plaintiff. This result clearly contradicts the basic postulate of effective judicial protection, in particular with regard to fundamental rights.

Less problematic appears to be the criterion of the *direct concern,* which will have to be, as a rule, affirmed in actions against directly effective decisions and regulations (unlike in case of directives, which need to be implemented), if the measure concerned shows its effects without the intervention of a – communitarian or national – act devoted to the implementation of such a measure. The legal situation is different when the measure at issue as such causes a still insufficiently precise intervention in the legal sphere of the plaintiff, but leaves the Member States or the Community institutions with a scope of discretion in the implementation.[290]

The criterion of *direct concern* represents an obstacle for individual actions, as a rule, in case of actions against directives. They need to be implemented by the Member States, whereupon a more or less wide scope of discretion remains with the national legislator. In normal case, therefore, a direct concern is not given in actions against directives. Exceptions can be considered only if the defendant, irrespective of its legal form, is attributable to the State in the broadest sense and, therefore, can be the addressee of the direct effect of the directive concerned. Consideration would thus have to be given – under the preconditions developed by the case-law of the ECJ –, for instance, to the local authorities, fiscal authorities, and also to the independent State authorities and public undertakings, which have been made responsible, pursuant to a measure adopted by the State, for providing public services under the control of the State, and have for that purpose special powers.[291]

The action for annulment can be based only on one of the four causes of action (*"moyens"*) enumerated in the Treaties, viz., lack of competence, infringement of an essential procedural requirement, infringement of the Treaties or of any rule of law relating to their application, or misuse of powers (Article 263(2) TFEU; ex-Article 230(2) TEC; ex-Article 146(2) Euratom Treaty). In connection with violations of the fundamental rights, especially the cause of action relating to the "infringement of the Treaties or of any rule of law relating to their application" needs to be highlighted. This generally means the infringement of the substantive Community/Union law, including the fundamental rights, which are applicable as

---

290 Judgement of 23.4.1986, Les Verts v European Parliament, ibid., 1367; judgement of 3.5.2002, Jégo-Quéré v Commission, ibid., II-2377; judgement of 27.6.2000, Salamander v Parliament and Council, Cases T-172/98, T-175/98 to T-177/98, EuGE 2000, II-2487, II-2513. As regards decisions, see: judgement of 1.7.1965, Töpfer, Joined Cases 106 and 107/63, ECR 1965, 548, 556; judgement of 23.11.1971, Bock, Case 62/70, ECR 1971, 897, 908; judgement of 11.7.1984, Gemeinde Differdange, Case 222/83, ECR 1984, 2889, 2896; judgement of 7.7.1987, Etoile commerciale and CNTA, Joined Cases 89 and 91/86, ECR 1987, 3005, 3025.As regards regulations, see: judgement of 13.5.1971, Fruit Company, Joined Cases 41-44/70, ECR 1971, 411, 422; judgement of 17.3.1987, Mannesmann, Case 333/85, ECR 1987, 1381, 1409; judgement of 26.6.1990, Sofrimport, Case C-152/88, ECR 1990, I-2477, I-2507.

291 Judgement of 12.7.1990, Foster v British Gas, Case C-188/89, ECR 1990, I-3313, I-3348 et seq.

general principles of Community/Union law. In such a case, the ECJ or the GC also examines whether the contested legal act is based on materially incorrect facts or an incorrect assessment of the facts.[292]

The action must be instituted within two months of the publication of the measure, or of its notification to the plaintiff, or, in the absence thereof, of the day on which it came to the knowledge of the plaintiff, as the case may be (Article 263(6) TFEU; ex-Article 230(5) TEC; ex-Article 146(5) Euratom Treaty).[293]

If the action is admissible and well founded, the ECJ or the GC shall declare the act concerned to be void (Article 264(1) TFEU; ex-Article 231(1) TEC; ex-Article 147(1) Euratom Treaty). The judgment annulling a measure is of constitutive nature; it remedies the improper legal act basically with *ex tunc* und *erga omnes* effect. However, the ECJ or the GC can, in exceptional cases, maintain, fully or partially, the effects of the annulled act in case it deems this to be necessary, in particular, in the interest of the legal certainty, the continuity of the regulation or for the protection of legitimate expectations of the persons concerned (Article 264(2) TFEU; ex-Article 231(2) TEC; ex-Article 147(2) Euratom Treaty).

6.1.4.1.2.3. Specificities of the action for failure to act

As already described above, the action for failure to act (Article 265 TFEU; ex-Article 232 TEC; ex-Article 148 Euratom Treaty) supplements the action for annulment in the system of legal protection under the Treaties in case the unlawful conduct of the Union's institution concerned, including the European Central Bank, consists in a failure to act (omission to take a decision).

The preconditions for the admissibility of an action for failure to act resemble those of the action for annulment: Member States and the Union's institutions need not prove any special interest in bringing an action. However, any natural or legal person could complain only "that an institution, body, office or agency of the Union has failed to address to that person any act other than a recommendation or an opinion" (Article 265(3) TFEU; ex-Article 232(3) TEC; ex-Article 148(3) Euratom Treaty). Actions brought by individuals for the enactment of normative

---

292 Judgement of 11.7.1984, Remia, Case 42/83, ECR 1985, 2545, 2570; judgement of 7.5.1987, Nachi Fujikoshi, Case 255/84, ECR 1987, 1861, 1890.

293 The period of two months is extended on account of distance by a single period of 10 days (Article 81 § 2 of the Rules of Procedure of the Court of Justice of the European Communities; Article 102 § 2 of the Rules of Procedure of the Court of First Instance of the European Communities). If the time-limit, including the extension on account of distance, expires on a Saturday or a Sunday or an official holiday, it shall be extended until the end of the first following working day (Article 80 § 2 of the Rules of Procedure of the Court of Justice of the European Communities; Article 101 § 2 of the Rules of Procedure of the Court of First Instance of the European Communities).

acts (regulations or directives) are, therefore, inadmissible because these could not be described as acts, which could be addressed to the plaintiff.[294]

As concerns the substantive division of jurisdiction between the ECJ and the GC, the statements already made with regard to actions for annulment apply analogously to the action for failure to act: such actions, which are brought by the Member States or Union's institutions, including the European Central Bank, should be, subject to certain exceptions, brought before the ECJ at the first and last instance. For actions for failure to act brought by other plaintiffs, the GC has jurisdiction at the first instance, whereupon an appeal, limited to questions of law, can be filed against its decisions before the ECJ (Article 256(2) TFEU; ex-Article 225(2) TEC; ex-Article 140a(2) Euratom Treaty in conjunction with Article 51(1, 2) of the Statute of the Court of Justice).

The action for failure to act is admissible only if the institution concerned has first been called upon to act, and if within two months of being so called upon, the institution concerned "has not defined its position". In such a case, the action may be brought within a further period of two months (Article 265(2) TFEU; ex-Article 232(2) TEC; ex-Article 148(2) Euratom Treaty).[295] However, if the institution has "defined its position", the way to the action for failure to act is blocked, and the request can, if need be, pursued further only with the action for annulment (Article 263 TFEU; ex-Article 230 TEC; ex-Article 146 Euratom Treaty) against the incriminating position.

Admittedly, the existing case-law does not guarantee with sufficient certainty that a refusal by the institution to act, which obstructs the way to an action for failure to act, is, in any case, voidable with the action for annulment.[296] Therefore, de lege ferenda, a drafting clarification is recommended to the effect that only the decisions, which are voidable by means of the action for annulment, should be

---

294 Judgement of 26.10.1971, Mackprang, Case 15/71, ECR 1971, 797, 804; judgement of 15.1.1974, Holtz & Willemsen, Case 134/73, ECR 1974, 1, 10; judgement of 28.3.1979, Granaria, Case 90/87, ECR 1979, 1081, 1093; Decision of 11.7.1979, Fédération Nationale des Producteurs de Vin de Table, Case 59/79, ECR 1979, 2425, 2433; judgement of 26.4.1988, Asteris and Greece v Commission, Joined Cases 97, 193, 199 and 215/86, ECR 1988, 2181, 2206.

295 The rules for the computation of the procedural time-limits for the actions for annulment are accordingly applicable for the computation of the time-limit for bringing an action for failure to act (see above).

296 Cf. judgement of 26.4.1988, Asteris and Greece v Commission, ibid., 2208. See also judgement of 18.10.1979, GEMA, Case 125/78, ECR 1979, 3173, 3190. The statement, in a recent judgement, which is inconsistent with the existing case-law, is incomprehensible, that even the explicit refusal to act does not affect the admissibility of the action for failure to act since it does not put an end to the failure to act: judgement of 27.9.1988, European Parliament v Council, "Comitology", Case 302/87, ECR 1988, 5615, 5641.

looked upon as "positions" within the meaning of Article 265(2) TFEU (ex-Article 232(2) TEC; ex-Article 148(2) Euratom Treaty).[297]

The final judgment on the merits, which concludes the proceedings, is a non-enforceable declaratory judgment; it establishes the infringement of the Treaties due to the omission in question by the defendant Union's institution. It is incumbent upon that institution – as it is incumbent upon the Member States in the Treaty infringement procedure –, "to take the necessary measures to comply with the judgment of the Court of Justice of the European Union" (Article 266(1) TFEU; ex-Article 233(1, 3) TEC; ex-Article 149(1) Euratom Treaty).

Unlike the action for annulment, the action for failure to act has hardly any practical significance. The reason for that may lie in the fact that a failure to act can be complained of as contrary to the Treaty only if the Union's institution concerned is under an obligation to act, which must be sufficiently specific in terms of scope and time. Therefore, this procedure is not suitable as an instrument for judicial enforcement of actions, for which the involved parties have scope of political discretion.[298]

6.1.4.1.2.4. Assessment of the cases with regard to the protection of fundamental rights

The violations of fundamental rights protected under the Union law could be brought before the court by means of the actions for annulment and for failure to act just as with the Treaty infringement procedure. In contrast to the Treaty infringement procedure, the actions for annulment and for failure to act are, however, directed against the unlawful acts or omissions of the Union's institutions and bodies, not of the Member States and their national entities.

The action for annulment and the action for failure to act differ from each other in that the former has as its object an unlawful act of a Union's institution, whereas the latter has as its object the failure of a Union's institution to act where there is a legal duty to do so. Both the actions supplement each other; they form an indivisible whole with the aim to achieve a complete review of the legality of the conduct of the Union's institutions. The effects of the respective judgment upholding the action are, however, different: In the annulment proceedings, a constitutive judgement is pronounced, in the action for failure to act, a declaratory judgement.

---

297 Cf. Manfred A. Dauses, Empfiehlt es sich, das System des Rechtsschutzes und der Gerichtsbarkeit in der Europäischen Gemeinschaft, insbesondere die Aufgaben der Gemeinschaftsgerichte und der nationalen Gerichte, weiterzuentwickeln? Gutachten zum 60. Deutschen Juristentag, Münster 1994, p. D-110.

298 Cf. judgement of 22.5.1985, European Parliament v Council, "Common transport policy", Case 13/83, ECR 1985, 1513, 1588.

Problems of demarcation could arise when the defendant Union's institution, despite having been called upon to do so, explicitly refuses to enact the requested Union act. In such a case, only the action for annulment may be of help against the refusal. On the other hand, the action for failure to act helps if the institution, despite having been called upon to act, remains completely inactive ("*recours en carence*").

Unlike in the Treaty infringement procedure, in the actions for annulment and for failure to act, not only the Commission or the Member States could, as the privileged "guardians of the Treaties", appear as the plaintiffs, but also other Union's institutions (including the European Central Bank), whose actions are, however, at least partially, admissible only insofar as they aim to protect their own rights. Furthermore, a court action may be brought by natural and legal persons as the "non-privileged applicants". They could bring an action only against Union acts, or for the enactment of Union acts, which are of direct and, generally, also of individual concern to them. The requirement of individual concern proves to be a high hurdle in the legal protection, which practically excludes actions against normative acts, or for the enactment of normative acts.

In summary, it can be stated that the actions for annulment and for failure to act not only fulfil legal supervisory functions, but also function as instruments for enforcing individual protective rights, the fundamental rights being in the forefront. Nevertheless, they perform a genuine function to protect individuals only to a restricted extent; for due to the admissibility criterion of direct and, in particular, individual concern, the natural or legal persons basically do not have any right to bring legal proceedings against genuine normative acts adopted by legislative procedure (legislative acts), such as regulations and directives.

6.1.4.1.3. Union actions for damages

6.1.4.1.3.1. Presentation of the cases (Generalities)

The Union law recognises two types of actions for damages, flowing from different sources of law, for an infringement of the Union law: the actions for liability of the Union, which are enshrined in the TFEU(formerly TEC and Euratom Treaty), based on the "non-contractual" (i.e., tortious) liability, which can be brought against the Union (including the European Central Bank) and its institutions and servants , and the – developed by the ECJ in its creative case-law – State liability actions, which are directed against the Member States and the individuals and entities attributable to them (so-called "Francovich" doctrine).

Both types of action have in common that they justify an objective liability without fault, primarily for legislative tort. The liability presupposes a "sufficiently qualified breach" of the Community/Union law, by which a manifest and grave infringement of the limits of power under the Community/Union law is understood. Such an *ultra vires* can also manifest itself in an infringement of the Union's fundamental rights.

Whereas the actions for liability of the Union (including the European Central Bank) should be brought before the institutional Union courts, namely the GC (at the first instance) and the ECJ (in the appeal proceedings) – whereby, the proceedings are governed by the Community/Union law –, the national courts have jurisdiction for the State liability actions, and the proceedings are governed by the national constitution of the courts and the national procedural law.

6.1.4.1.3.2. Specificities of the action for liability of the Union

Pursuant to Article 268 in conjunction with Article 340(2) TFEU (ex-Article 235 in conjunction with ex-Article 288(2) TEC; ex-Article 151 in conjunction with ex-Article 188(2) Euratom Treaty), the ECJ or, at the first instance, the GC has the jurisdiction to hear the actions for damages based on the "non-contractual" (i.e., tortious) liability of the Union. In this area, "the Union shall, in accordance with the general principles common to the laws of the Member States, make good any damage caused by its institutions or by its servants in the performance of their duties". Since the amendment by the Maastricht Treaty on European Union, the same is applicable for any damage caused by the European Central Bank or its servants in the performance of their duties (Article 340(3) TFEU; ex-Article 288(3) TEC).

The action for liability of the Union is similar to a *recours de pleine juridiction*, that is, the ECJ or the GC can determine the amount of the damages to be paid according to the respective circumstances. The reference to the common European principles of law to be inferred from the legal orders of the Member States enshrines an authority conferred on the Union courts to elaborate the elements of liability under the Union law by further developing this law.

The action for liability of the Union follows autonomous criteria. According to the established case-law, it is an independent form of action with a particular purpose and specific preconditions, which differs from the actions for annulment and for failure to act in that its objective is not the abolition of a particular measure, but compensation for damage caused by a Union institution.[299] In this respect, the action for liability has proven to be an advantageous supplementation of the actions

299 Judgement of 28.4.1971, Lütticke, Case 4/69, ECR 1971, 325, 337; judgement of 2.7.1974, Holtz & Willemsen, Case 153/73, ECR 1974, 675, 694; judgement of 17.12.1981, Ludwigshafener Walzmühle, Joined Cases 197-200, 243, 245 and 247/80, ECR 1981, 3211, 3246; judgement of 15.5.1990, Sonito, Case C-87/89, ECR 1990, I-1981, I-2010.

for annulment and for failure to act, as it is the only type of action by means of which the natural or legal persons could bring legal proceedings against a normative act or omission of a Union's institution directly before the institutional Union courts, the ECJ or the GC. Therewith, it performs a specific function in the Union's system of legal protection; it helps in counterbalancing, at least partially, the restrictions on the right of the natural and legal persons to bring legal proceedings within the scope of actions for annulment and for failure to act.

In practice, particular attention is given to the liability of the Union for normative (legislative) injustice. According to the established case-law, a liability on account of a legislative measure, which involves choices of economic policy, cannot be incurred, unless a sufficiently qualified breach of a superior rule of law for the protection of the individual has occurred, to which also belong the general principles of law – in particular, the fundamental rights –, which are integrating elements of the Union's legal order.[300]

With the requirement of the "sufficiently qualified breach" when making choices of economic policy, the liability is substantially limited to cases in which the Union's institution (or the European Central Bank) has "manifestly and gravely" disregarded the limits on the exercise of its powers, without being able to cite grounds of important public interests therefore.[301] The strict application of this qualificative results in that, despite the "no-fault" character of the liability[302], statistically less than 10% of the actions for damages are successful.

The action for damages is modelled as a purely judicial procedure; preliminary administrative proceedings are not required.

Bringing a court action is not bound to any procedural time-limits. However, claims arising from a non-contractual liability are barred after a period of five years from the occurrence of the event giving rise thereto. The period of limitation

300 Judgement of 2.12.1971, Schöppenstedt, Case 5/71, ECR 1971, 975, 985; judgement of 14.5.1975, CNTA, Case 74/74, ECR 1975, 533, 546; judgement of 2.6.1976, Kampffmeyer, Joined Cases 56-60/74, ECR 1976, 711, 744; judgement of 25.5.1978, HNL, Joined Cases 83 and 94/76, 4, 15 and 40/77, ECR 1978, 1209, 1224; judgement of 4.10.1979, Interquell Stärke-Chemie, Joined Cases 261 and 262/78, ECR 1979, 3045, 3064; judgement of 30.5.1989, Roquette Frères, Case 20/88, ECR 1989, 1553, 1586; judgement of 6.6.1990, AERPO, Case C-119/88, ECR 1990, I-2189, I-2211; judgement of 19.5.1992, Mulder and Heinemann, Joined Cases C-104/89 and C-37/90, ECR 1992, I-3061, I-3131.

301 Judgement of 25.5.1978, HNL, ibid., 1245, judgement of 26.6.1990, Sofrimport, Case 152/80, ECR 1990, I-2477, I-2511; judgement of 19.5.1992, Mulder and Heinemann, ibid., I-3132.

302 Cf. judgement of 10.7.1969, Sayag, Case 9/69, ECR 1969, 329, 335; judgement of 28.4.1971, Lütticke, ibid., 337; judgement of 2.7.1974, Holtz & Willemsen, ibid., 693; judgement of 14.5.1975, CNTA, ibid., 549; judgement of 25.5.1978, HNL, ibid., 1232.

is interrupted, if proceedings are instituted before the ECJ (or the GC) or if an application is made to the relevant Union's institution.[303]

6.1.4.1.3.3. Specificities of the action for State liability

The Union Treaties enshrine provisions concerning the liability of the Union itself, as well as the liability of the European Central Bank in the event of an infringement of the Union law. However, the Treaties did not make any provisions for the liability of the Member States in the event of infringements of the Union law. Consequently, if the institutions or the servants of a Member State or one of its public bodies infringe the primary or secondary Union law or the general principles of law recognised in the Union legal order, in particular, the fundamental rights, and, thereby, cause a damage, then, in such a case, no explicit basis of liability can be inferred from the Union Treaties. The development and shaping of a uniform Union doctrine of State liability in case of an infringement of the Union law by the Member States was, therefore, left to the praetorian law-making by the ECJ.

The line of case-law historically initiated by the *leading case* "Francovich and Bonifaci" (1991)[304] affirms a claim seeking to establish State liability under Community law (now: Union law) in case of serious infringements of Union law by a Member State, whereby these may be infringements of the obligation to implement directives, as well as other infringements of Union law, such as violations of Union's fundamental rights. The claim for compensation is, insofar the brief and apodictic grounds of the judgment show, inferred from the principle of effectiveness ("*effet utile*") of the Union law, and is conceived as a compensation for the lack of enforceability of the rights conferred by Union law, whereby the lack of enforceability is caused by the failure of the Member State. It is virtually the pertinent supplementation of the direct effect of the Union's provisions on the

303 Article 46 of the Statute of the Court of Justice. Concerning the start of the period of limitation: judgement of 27.1.1982, Birra Wührer, Joined Cases 256, 257, 265 and 267/80, as well as 5/81, ECR 1982, 85, 106; judgement of 27.1.1982, De Franceschi, Case 51/81, ECR 1982, 117, 134. It has not been finally clarified whether the expiry of the period of limitation is to be observed officially or only on pleas of the defendant Community/Union institution (or the European Central Bank).

304 Judgement of 19.11.1991, Francovich, Bonifaci and others, Joined Cases C-6/90 and C-9/90, ECR 1991, I-5357. This *cause célèbre* was based on the fact that Italy had not implemented the Directive 80/987/EEC of 20.10.1980 (so-called "Insolvency Directive", OJ. 1980, L 283/23) in Italian law within the prescribed period, which is why the plaintiff employees could not enforce the salary claims, which they had against their insolvent employer.

infringement of which the damage caused is based.[305] For this purpose, the ECJ succinctly states:[306]

> "The full effectiveness of Community rules would be impaired and the protection of the rights which they grant would be weakened if individuals were unable to demand reparation when their rights are infringed by a breach of Community law for which a Member State can be held responsible.
> The possibility of reparation by the Member State is particularly indispensable where the full effectiveness of Community rules, as is in the present case, is subject to prior action on the part of the State and where, consequently, in the absence of such action, individuals cannot enforce before the national courts the rights conferred upon them by Community law.
> It follows that the principle whereby a State must be liable for loss and damage caused to individuals by breaches of Community law for which the State can be held responsible is inherent in the system of the Treaty."

Unlike the national law of most of the Member States, the communitarian State liability law (now: Union's State liability Law) also includes the liability for legislative injustice. It is based on the principle of objective liability, i.e., the obligation to compensate for the damages is not linked to any element of fault whatsoever (intent or negligence), rather is rooted in the objective wrongful conduct of the State.

In several subsequent judgements, the modalities of liability have been specified more precisely. Accordingly, the State liability under Union law intervenes, if the following preconditions are fulfilled:[307]

- The Union law confers subjective rights upon individuals.
- The Member State concerned has "manifestly and gravely" disregarded the limits on the exercise of its powers and, thereby, has breached the Union law in a sufficiently serious manner. This happens to be the case, in particular, when a directive is not implemented properly, furthermore, when a judgement pronounced in the Treaty infringement procedure or in the preliminary ruling

305 Judgement of 5.3.1996, Brasserie du Pêcheur and Factortame, Joined Cases C-46/93 and C-48/93, ECR 1996, I-1029, I-1143.

306 Judgement of 19.11.1991, Francovich, Bonifaci and others, ibid., I-5414.

307 Judgement of 16.12.1993, Wagner Miret, Case C-334/92, ECR 1993, I-6911; judgement of 5.3.1996, Brasserie du Pêcheur and Factortame, ibid.; judgement of 26.3.1996, British Telecommunications, Case C-392/93, ECR 1996, I-163; judgement of 23.5.1996, Hedley Lomas, Case C-5/94, ECR 1996, I-2553; judgement of 8.10.1996, MP Travel Line, Case C-178/94, ECR 1996, I-4845; judgement of 17.10.1996, Denkavit, Joined Cases C-283/94, C-291/94 and C-292/94, ECR 1996, I-5063; judgement of 30.9.2003, Köbler, Case C-224/01, ECR 2003, I-10239.

procedure is not observed or in case of derogation from an established relevant case-law of the ECJ in some other manner.[308]
- The person concerned has incurred a damage as a result of a breach of obligation by the Member State (causal link).

A large number of judgements pertain to the non- or mis-implementation of directives. This is not the only area in which the State liability is applicable. Rather, any sufficiently qualified breach of Union law is adequate, irrespective of whether the breach, which gave rise to the damage, is attributable to the legislature, the judiciary or the executive of the Member State concerned. Thereby, the preconditions for liability must, in principle, be the same as those under which the Union's institutions incur liability in a comparable situation.

In the event the preconditions for liability exist, as defined by the Union law, the claim for compensation on the merits arises directly from the Union law. Unlike the actions for damages against the Union, which are explicitly assigned to the jurisdiction of the GC/ECJ, the actions for damages against the Member States should be brought before the national courts, which have jurisdiction according to the national law. Therewith, the modalities for the assertion of the claim are, in principle, governed by the conditions for the reparation of loss and damage (compensation law) laid down by the respective Member State, in particular, concerning the determination of the jurisdiction of the courts and for laying down the procedural rules for proceedings. Admittedly, in doing so, two mandatory requirements of the Union law should be observed, namely that the formal and material conditions for the claim must not be less favourable than those relating to similar purely domestic actions (prohibition on less favourable treatment), and it may not be made in practice impossible or excessively difficult for the individual to obtain reparation (prohibition on frustrating the objectives of the claim).[309]

6.1.4.1.3.4. Assessment of the cases with regard to the protection of fundamental rights

The actions for damages are conceived as procedures for the judicial protection of individual rights. The natural and legal persons, who assert the violation of their

308 Judgement of 5.3.1996, Brasserie du Pêcheur and Factortame, ibid., I-1150. The additional criteria, which the national courts have to take into consideration when assessing the existence of the conditions for liability, are, among others, the clarity and precision of the rule breached, the measure of discretion left by that rule to the national or Community authorities, and whether the infringement and the damage caused were intentional or involuntary (ibid.).

309 Judgement of 19.11.1991, Francovich, Bonifaci and others, ibid., I-5416.

rights, especially the fundamental rights protected under the Union's legal order, have the right to bring legal proceedings, also insofar as the asserted violation was caused by a normative act or by the omission to enact a normative act. Therewith, this procedure has a close substantive connection with the actions for annulment and for failure to act, which are directed at the annulment and/or the enactment of binding Union acts.

If, in the latter procedures, natural or legal persons appear as the plaintiffs, their right to bring legal proceedings is, above all, restricted by the admissibility criterion of individual concern (cf. Point 6.1.4.1.2. above). The actions for damages, which enable the individuals to defend themselves also against the normative injustice, counterbalance, at least partially, this restriction.

Actions for damages should, therefore, be categorised especially as "individual protection-friendly". This is valid not only theoretically, but is seen also in practice: just in the area of Union liability procedures, individual actions against normative acts, above all, against the regulations in the field of agricultural policy, are characteristic.

It is to be noted that only the actions for damages due to the infringements of Union law by the Union itself could be brought before the Union's courts, GC/ECJ ("non-contractual liability", Article 268 in conjunction with Article 340(2) TFEU; ex-Article 235 in conjunction with ex-Article 288(2) TEC; ex-Article 151 in conjunction with ex-Article 188(2) Euratom Treaty). The second category of procedures, which relate to the infringements of Union law by the Member States and the institutions and entities attributable to them, can be brought before the national courts, whereby the Union law only dictates the framework, whereas the substantive modalities, as well as the procedure are defined by the national law (doctrine of State liability "Francovich").

In summary, it can be noted that the actions for damages (both in the form of procedures concerning non-contractual liability of the Union, as well as the State liability procedures) constitute beneficial instruments for the protection of individuals, but, according to the subject matter of their action and the possible content of the judgements, have an inherent unmistakable shortcoming vis-à-vis the Treaty infringement procedure and vis-à-vis the actions for annulment and for failure to act: although by means of the actions for liability, an indemnification can be asserted *a posteriori*, i.e., the damage suffered can be compensated, however, the existence of the unlawful Union or national law is not directly affected thereof. Consequently, in the final analysis, these actions prove to be unsuitable to remedy the violations of fundamental rights as such.

6.1.4.2. Preliminary ruling procedure

6.1.4.2.1. Presentation of the case (Generalities)

The preliminary ruling procedure (Article 267 TFEU; ex-Article 234 TEC; ex-Article 150 Euratom Treaty), a cornerstone of the Union's system of legal protection, is not a stand-alone type of action, but an incidental procedure in a dispute pending before a Member State court. As a "sourced-out interlocutory procedure"[310], it is based on the basic principles of the separation of functions and cooperation between the national trial courts and the ECJ. It establishes the link to the national courts, and thus creates a procedural interface between the national law and the Union law. Its paramount importance for the legal practice is owed to the circumstance that both the legal circles increasingly influence and penetrate each other, and that the economic, social and political life in the Member States is increasingly integrated in the Union's network of relationships.

In the preliminary ruling procedure, the ECJ (not the GC!) has jurisdiction, upon presentation by a national trial court, to decide on the questions of Union law, which have been raised within the scope of a legal dispute pending with the latter.[311] Consequently, unlike the above described direct actions, the preliminary ruling procedure is not a litigation in itself, but functionally an element of the legal dispute pending before the referring national court, within the scope of which the

---

310 Georg Ress, Die Entscheidungserheblichkeit im Vorlageverfahren nach Artikel 177 EWGV im Vergleich zum Vorlageverfahren nach Artikel 100 Abs. 1 GG, in: Festschrift für Günter Jahr, 1993, p. 339.

311 Altogether, almost half of all the legal disputes decided by the ECJ since 1952 trace back to the requests for preliminary rulings by the Member States' courts. Typically, just the most significant decisions, in terms of legal history, of the ECJ have been pronounced, without exception, in this type of procedure, thus, for instance, the groundbreaking judgements on the direct application and primacy of the Community law, on the Member State liability, on the fundamental freedoms of the common market/internal market and, *last but not least*, on the fundamental rights. The law-making power of these judgements and their precedence-creating influence have decisively contributed to shaping the Community legal order as an autonomous legal system with its own structural and guiding principles. Cf. Manfred A. Dauses, Das Vorabentscheidungsverfahren nach Artikel 177 EG-Vertrag, 2nd edition 1995, p. 50 et seqq., idem, Az elözetes döntéshozatali eljárás az EK Szerzödés 177-es cikke szerint (Hungarian translation of the above-mentioned book), Budapest 2000, p. 42 et seqq. See also: Ulrich Everling, das Vorabentscheidungsverfahren vor dem Gerichtshof der Europäischen Gemeinschaften, 1986; Reimer Voß, Erfahrungen und Probleme bei der Anwendung des Vorabentscheidungsverfahrens nach Art. 177 EWGV, in: EuR 1986, p. 95.

ECJ, as the central institutional Union's court, *ex ante* clarifies the questions of Union law, which are anticipatable for the outcome of the starting dispute.

Similar to an appeals procedure, a preliminary ruling procedure performs, besides the legal protection function, an important coordination function. However, it differs from an appeals procedure in that it does not serve as any amendment of an already pronounced decision, but intends to give the national court useful information on the existence and content of the relevant Union law before it pronounces its judgement. As a result, it is not based on the hierarchical super- and subordination of the judicial institutions of the same type of court, but on the principle of cooperation and functionally separated interaction of equal-ranking courts with the objective to ensure the protection of Union law at all levels of the life in society.

Article 267 TFEU envisages a direct cooperation between the ECJ and the national courts within the scope of a non-contentious procedure. The cooperative function of this procedure results in that the decision on the referral to the Court of Justice is exclusively the matter of the trial court, and not of the parties to the main proceedings. Solely the trial court determines the questions to be referred; the parties (or the public prosecutor's office) could not change anything concerning the existence and wording of these questions. For this purpose, the ECJ has stated in the judgement in Singer[312] case:

> "Under Article 177 of the Treaty (now: Article 267 TFEU), it is for the court or tribunal of a Member State, and not the parties to the main action, to bring a matter before the Court of Justice. Since the right to determine the questions to be brought before the court thus devolves upon the court or tribunal of the Member State alone, the parties may not change their tenor or have them declared to be without purpose. Consequently, the Court of Justice cannot be compelled at the request of a party to entertain a question when the initiative for referring it to the court pertains not to the parties but to the court or tribunal of the Member State itself ... Besides, the contrary view fails to recognize that the authors of Article 177 intended to establish direct co-operation between the Court of Justice and the courts and tribunals of the Member States by way of a non-contentious procedure excluding any initiative of the parties, who are merely invited to be heard in the course of that procedure."

However, this does not exclude that the national trial courts open the possibility for the parties to the main proceedings to suggest a specific question, and that judicial remedies against any dismissal of their application are given according to the national law.[313]

312 Judgement of 9.12.1965, Singer, Case 44/65, ECR 1965, 1267, 1275.

313 Judgement of 12.2.1974, Rheinmühlen Düsseldorf, Case 146/73, ECR 1974, 139. The procedural court cannot, in any case, refer the parties to bring the matter before the Court of Justice: judgement of 12.5.1964, Wagner, Case 101/63, ECR 1964, 417, 430;

6.1.4.2.2. The concept of national courts

The preliminary ruling procedure can be initiated only by the courts, not by the administrative authorities, the public prosecutor's office or even private individuals. The Union Treaties do not define as to what is meant by a "court or tribunal" within this meaning. According to the established case-law of the ECJ, it is essential for the term "court or tribunal" that it is, whatever it may be called, an independent government body, which is not bound by instructions, for the settlement of disputes with binding jurisdiction.[314] This includes, for example, professional chambers, if they exercise the powers to resolve disputes,[315] furthermore, collective agreement arbitration boards, which by virtue of legal provisions decide on the disputes between the parties to a collective agreement, in case the collective agreement lacks special provisions.[316]

However, arbitration boards, which are established privately by an autonomous arbitration agreement between the parties, are excluded.[317] Since they do not exercise any State judicial function and, consequently, lack the integration into the general system of legal protection of the Member States, they could not claim the legal assistance of the ECJ. Thereby, the hostility of the Court of Justice primarily seems to be directed against the possibility of a manipulation of the procedure by private parties.[318]

6.1.4.2.3. Right to refer and obligation to refer

The principle of procedural economy and the principle of cooperation, which form the basis of the preliminary ruling procedure, require that the national trial court may refer a case to the ECJ only if it realises the relevance of the Union law ques-

---

cf. Order of 18.10.1979, Sirena, Case 40/70, ECR 1979, 169; Order of 14.7.1971, Rheinmühlen Düsseldorf, Case 6/71, ECR 1971, 719; judgement of 15.6.1972, Fratelli Grassi, Case 5/72, ECR 1972, 443. According to the German procedural law, although the parties could suggest a referral to the ECJ, however, an appeal against the refusal is not admissible.

314 Judgement of 30.6.1966, Vaassen-Göbbels, Case 61/65, ECR 1966, 583; cf. also judgement of 11.6.1987, Pretore di Salò, Case 14/86, ECR 1987, 2545; judgement of 23.3.1982, Nordsee, Case 102/81,ECR 1982, 1095.

315 Judgement of 6.10.1981, Broekmeulen, Case 246/80,ECR 1981, 2311, 2328 (for the Dutch Appeals Committee for General Medicine); Order of 18.6.1980, Borker, Case 138/80,ECR 1980, 1975 (for the French Conseil de l'Ordre des Avocats, which does not have any authority to decide disputes, but is authorised only to give opinions).

316 Judgement of 17.10.1989, Danfoss, Case 109/88, ECR 1989, 3220, 3224.

317 Judgement of 23.3.1982, Nordsee, ibid.

318 Cf. judgements of 11.3.1980 and of 16.12.1981, Foglia/Novello, Case 104/79, ECR 1980, 745, or Case 244/80, ECR 1981, 3045.

tions concerned within the scope of the legal dispute pending with it. According to the established judicial practice of the ECJ, in principle, it is for the national courts to review the relevance of such a question to the outcome of the action; the national court alone can determine both the relevance and the need to refer a question for a preliminary ruling and, therefore, has a wide "power of appraisal"[319] when deciding on the "whether" to refer and on the wording of the question to be referred.

The ECJ reviews the right to refer only in exceptional cases, and within narrow limits, in order to restrain a misuse of the procedure and, in particular, to rule out a referral purely for an expert opinion. Thereby, it places in the limelight the principle of cooperation and the function of inter-court assistance of the preliminary ruling procedure, which are opposed to the referral of purely hypothetical questions that are irrelevant for the decision of the dispute.[320]

The referral by the trial court can be optional or obligatory. National courts, "against whose decisions there is no judicial remedy under national law .... shall bring the matter before the Court" (Article 267(3) TFEU; ex-Article 234(3) TEC; ex-Article 150(3) Euratom Treaty), if they have a "reasonable doubt" with regard to a preliminary question of the Union law which is relevant for the decision.[321]

---

319 Judgement of 16.12.1981, Foglia/Novello II, Case 244/80, ibid., 3062; similarly judgement of 30.4.1986, Asjes, Joined Cases 209-213/84, ECR 1986, 1425, 1460; judgement of 26.9.1996, Allain, Case C-341/94, ECR 1996, I-4631, I-4654; judgement of 29.10.1998, Awoyemi, Case C-230/94, ECR 1998, I-6781, I-6808.

320 Order of 27.6.1979, Tribunal d'Instance Hayange, Case 105/79, ECR 1979, 2257; Order of 12.3.1980, Tribunal d'Instance Hayange, Case 60/80, ECR 1980, 771; judgement of 11.3.1980, Foglia/Novello I, Case 104/79, ibid., 760; judgement of 16.12.1981, Foglia/Novello II, Case 244/80, ibid., 3062; judgement of 16.9.1982, Vlaeminck, Case 132/81, ECR 1982, 2953, 2964; judgement of 28.11.1991, Durighello, Case C-186/90, ECR 1991, I-5773, I-5795 et seq.; judgement of 16.7.1992, Meilicke, Case C-83/91, ECR 1992, I-4871, I-4871; judgement of 26.1.1993, Telemarsicabruzzo, Joined Cases C-320/90 – C-322/90, ECR 1993, I-393, I-426; Order of 19.3.1993, Banchero, Case C-157/92, ECR 1993, I-1085.

321 Judgement of 6.10.1982, C.I.L.F.I.T., Case 283/81, ECR 1982, 3415, 3428 et seqq. Theoretically, a non-compliance by a national court with its obligation to make a reference can be the subject matter of an infringement procedure before the ECJ. However, for reasons of expediency, the Commission has refrained from bringing the review procedure in such case until now. Therewith, it is not ruled out that already the national law links sanctions to an infringement of the obligation to refer. Thus, for instance, the German law qualifies such a non-compliance as an infringement of the constitutional guarantee of the "lawful judge", which is enshrined in the German Basic Law (Article 101(1) 2nd sentence Basic Law (GG)); the individuals concerned could defend themselves against it by means of a constitutional complaint (Article 93(1) (4a) Basic Law (GG)). However, a guarantee, which is given under the German law, of the "lawful judge" only protects from "objective arbitrariness",

The courts other than those of last instance "may" present preliminary questions of Union law for preliminary ruling, if they consider that a decision on the question is necessary to enable them to give judgment (Article 267(2) TFEU; ex-Article 234(2) TEC; Article 150(2) Euratom Treaty).[322]

Over and above the wording of the relevant provisions, according to the case-law of the ECJ, even the courts other than those of last instance are obligated to make a reference whenever they deem a provision of Union law, which is relevant for the decision, to be invalid and, therefore, do not wish to apply it; in this respect, the ECJ claims to have the monopolistic power of rejection ("Foto-Frost" doctrine).[323]

---

not from the errors of law. In the relevant cases, the failure to refer concerned the conscious derogation by German courts from an established case-law of the ECJ: See Orders of the Federal Constitutional Court (BVerfG) of 8.4.1987, 2 BvR 687/85; of 4.11.1987, 2 BvR 763/85; of 4.11.1987, BvR 876/85; of 9.11.1987, 2 BvR 808/82.

322 The ECJ has not sufficiently clarified till this day whether the concept of the procedural courts of last instance is to be understood concretely or abstractly. An *obiter dictum* from the earlier case-law (judgement of 15.7.1964, Costa v ENEL, Case 6/64, ECR 1964, 1251, 1268), however, seems to suggest that the Court of Justice rather leans towards the concrete point of view. According to the concrete (functional) point of view, the obligation to refer is determined according to the type of procedure, i.e., a court is always bound to refer, if no further appeal is possible against its concrete decision due to the special nature of the pending legal dispute (e.g., the amount in dispute). However, according to the abstract (institutional) point of view, exclusively the hierarchically superior courts are obligated to make a reference. They are, e.g., in the Federal Republic of Germany, the Federal Constitutional Court (cf. BVerfGE vol. 37, p. 271, 281), and the five highest federal courts of law (Bundesgerichtshof (Federal Court of Justice), Bundesverwaltungsgericht (Federal Administrative Court), Bundesfinanzhof (Federal Tax Court), Bundesarbeitsgericht (Federal Employment Court), Bundessozialgericht (Federal Social Court).

323 Judgement of 22.10.1987, Foto-Frost, Case 314/85, ECR 1987, 4199, 4230. According to this ruling, the national procedural courts could review the validity of a Union act (and accordingly also an act of the ECB), on their own responsibility, and declare the act concerned to be valid. However, they are not empowered to declare the acts of the Union's institutions (and accordingly the acts of the ECB) to be invalid. An exception is applicable only for the courts, which act within the scope of a procedure to grant temporary legal protection (judgement of 21.2.1991, Zuckerfabrik Süderdithmarschen, Joined Cases C-143/88 and C-92/89, ECR 1991, I-415, I-542). In this case, the procedural court is empowered to grant a stay of execution of a national administrative act based on a Union regulation, if it has considerable doubts on the validity of that Union regulation, if the stay is necessary to prevent serious and irreparable damage, and if the Court, at the same time, refers to the ECJ the question of the validity of the relevant Union law for a preliminary ruling.

6.1.4.2.4. Issues eligible for referral

The questions concerned, which are amenable to referral in the preliminary ruling procedure, can be classified in two main groups (Article 267(1,2) TFEU; ex-Article 234(1, 2) TEC; ex-Article 150(1, 2) Euratom Treaty):

- Questions pertaining to the interpretation of the Union Treaties, i.e., of the primary Union law; the questions pertaining to the existence and substance of the general principles of the Union law, in particular, the fundamental rights recognised in the Union legal order, are on equal terms;[324]
- Questions pertaining to the validity and interpretation of the acts of the institutions of the Union and the European Central Bank. Among these count, for instance, regulations, directives, decisions and international agreements of the Union or the European Central Bank, and also – unlike in the action for annulment – non-binding acts of the institutions of the Union or the European Central Bank, such as recommendations, opinions, action programmes, declarations etc. The same may apply for the decisions of the representatives of the governments of the Member States within the Council, which directly relate to the realisation of the objectives of the Treaties.[325]

An analysis of the aforementioned groups of questions concerned, which are amenable to referral, shows that as regards subject matter, the scope of application of the preliminary ruling procedure is strictly limited to the interpretation and the review of the validity of the legal rules set out in the Union law. Therewith, those questions are cut out, which are to be attributed to the sphere of the application of law. This means, in particular, that in the preliminary ruling procedure the ECJ

- cannot decide on the application of the Union law to the subject matter of the main proceedings; the application of the law to reach a decision on the dispute

324 E.g., judgement of 12.1.1969, Stauder, Case 29/69, ECR 1969, 419, 424; judgement of 17.12.1970, Internationale Handelsgesellschaft, Case 11/70, ECR 1970, 1125, 1135; judgement of 14.5.1974, Nold, Case 4/73, ECR 1974, 491, 507; judgement of 13.12.1979, Hauer, Case 44/79, ECR 1979, 3727, 3744; judgement of 11.7.1989, Schräder, Case 265/87, ECR 1989, 2237, 2267; judgement of 13.7.1989, Wachauf, Case 5/88, ECR 2609, 2639.

325 Cf. Manfred A. Dauses, Das Vorabentscheidungsverfahren nach Artikel 177 EG-Vertrag, ibid., p. 55 et seqq.

is, within the scope of the cooperation institutionalised by Article 267 TFEU, rather exclusively incumbent upon the referring national court;[326]

- cannot interpret national law or review its validity and/or applicability;[327]
- cannot decide on the compatibility of the national law with the Union law.[328]

6.1.4.2.5. Assessment of the case with regard to the protection of fundamental rights

The purpose of the preliminary ruling procedure is primarily to guarantee the substantive unity and cohesion of the Union, as well as the uniform interpretation of the Union law in all the Member States. The procedure helps to coordinate the case-law of the national courts in the area of Community/Union law, whereby it should be guaranteed that "the Community character of the law established by the Treaty is preserved … [and] that this law always has the same effect in all the Member States of the Community."[329]

The individual rights-protecting function of the preliminary ruling procedure is only of limited effectiveness. Although this procedure constitutes an advantageous supplementation of the direct actions, in particular, the actions for annulment and for failure to act, which are brought by natural or legal persons, however, according to its basic structure, it offers no full functional compensation for the restricted right of the individuals to bring legal proceedings within the scope of the aforementioned contradictory procedures.

Thus, first of all, the referral to the ECJ is basically optional, and only in exceptional cases, obligatory (courts of last instance, Article 267(3) TFEU; "Foto-Frost" doctrine). Moreover, the preliminary reference procedure is formed as *inter iudices* procedure, which means that alone the national court, and not the parties to the main proceedings, has to decide on the "whether" to refer and on the wording of the question to be referred; the parties to the proceedings could only give suggestions in this regard.

Especially with regard to the question referred and the preliminary ruling of the ECJ, it is to be noted that both could relate only abstractly to the substance of

326 Judgement of 27.3.1963, Da Costa and others, Joined Cases 28-30/62, ECR 1963, 63, 81; judgement of 15.7.1964, Costa v ENEL, Case 6/64, ECR 1964, 1251, 1268.

327 Judgement of 20.2.1973, Fonderie Officine Riunite, Case 54/72, ECR 1973, 193, 205; judgement of 17.6.1975, Mr and Mrs F., Case 7/75, ECR 1975, 679, 689; judgement of 13.3.1984, Prantl, Case 16/83, ECR 1984, 1299, 1324; judgement of 12.7.1984, Klopp, Case 107/83, ECR 1984, 2971, 2988.

328 Judgement of 13.3.1986, Mirepoix, Case 54/85, ECR 1986, 1067, 1076; judgement of 11.6.1987, Pretore di Salò, Case 14/86, ECR 1987, 2545, 2569; judgement of 22.9.1988, Pretura Unificata Turin, Case 228/87, ECR 1988, 5099, 5119.

329 Judgement of 16.1.1974, Rheinmühlen Düsseldorf, Case 166/73, ECR 1974, 33, 38.

the Union law. On the one hand, only the Union law, not the national law, can be the subject of a reference; on the other hand, the reference can pertain only to the interpretation and/or the review of the validity of the Union law, and not its application to reach a decision on the dispute.

The overall conclusion is that the preliminary ruling procedure as an abstract, non-litigious interlocutory procedure, which is based on the direct cooperation of courts without any noteworthy codetermination rights of the parties, in particular, in the initiation and execution of the procedure, fails to meet the expectations for an effective protection of individual rights.

6.1.5. Ways to improve the institutional protection of fundamental rights

6.1.5.1. Preliminary remark

The preceding overview of the most important types of actions and judgements shows that the Union's system of legal protection, in its existing form, is incomplete with regard to the protection of fundamental rights and, therefore, is in need of adjustment and supplementation. This condition has not intrinsically changed, since the Lisbon Reform Treaty has entered into force. Although this Treaty enshrines a cross-reference to the European Charter of Fundamental Rights (Article 6(1) TEU, new version), however, fails to create special rules for the institutional legal protection in case of violations of the fundamental rights granted in the Union. Only Article 263(4) TFEU entails a substantial innovation in the system of legal protection: henceforth, natural or legal persons shall be able to bring actions for annulment against the regulatory acts, which are of direct (but not necessarily individual) concern to the plaintiff, if those acts do not entail implementing measures.

The statements made below are restricted to an analysis of the applicable law. Therewith, the question is raised, what adjustments and supplementations to the current system of legal protection are needed in order to guarantee an adequate protection of fundamental rights. In this analysis, the author assumes that, as far as possible, overlapping remedies should be avoided and that, therefore, it should be examined, first of all, whether a situation, which is compatible with the fundamental rights, can be created by an amendment to the existing types of procedures and judgements, before the introduction of a new, fundamental rights-specific legal institution, namely an autonomous fundamental rights complaint, is recommended. In our opinion, such a fundamental rights complaint should only be contemplated, if the existing structure of legal protection, if need be, provided with certain modifications, proves to be insufficient or ineffective to ensure that the Union's fundamental rights are respected by the institutions and bodies of the Union, as well as by the Member States when implementing Union law.

On the basis of these preliminary remarks, three categories of procedures can be distinguished with regard to their contribution to the institutional protection of fundamental rights:

- procedures, which, according to their function and structure, are not suitable for an autonomous protection of individual fundamental rights;
- procedures, which could, in a modified form, be suitable for an autonomous protection of fundamental rights;
- a fundamental rights complaint as a specific instrument for the protection of fundamental rights.

6.1.5.2. Procedures, which are not suitable for an autonomous protection of fundamental rights

In this connection, those procedures are considered, which are not suitable, without changing their substance, as instruments for an effective protection of fundamental rights.

6.1.5.2.1. Union actions for damages

The action for damages directed against the Union (Article 268 in conjunction with Article 340(2,3) TFEU; ex-Article 235 in conjunction with Article 288(2) TEC; ex-Article 151 in conjunction with Article 188(2) Euratom Treaty), or the State liability action (according to the "Francovich" doctrine), in case it is admissible and well founded, leads to a judgment granting affirmative relief ("Leistungsurteil"), in which the defendant is ordered to pay compensation for the damage caused by it in violation of the Union law. The compensation is provided a *posteriori* for the suffered violations and damages.

The improper act or the improper omission itself, which gave rise to the obligation to pay compensation for damages, is not directly affected by the judgment granting affirmative relief. Consequently, the aforementioned procedures are not directed at the elimination of any violation, *in casu* of a violation of fundamental rights; they fail to qualify as autonomous instruments for protection against violations of fundamental rights.

6.1.5.2.2. Preliminary ruling procedure

In the preliminary ruling procedure (Article 267 TFEU; ex-Article 234 TEC; ex-Article 150 Euratom Treaty), the ECJ decides on the reference made by a Member State trial court concerning the existence or substance of Union law, including the fundamental rights, which are applicable as general principles of the Union law. The specific legal dispute is not decided in this type of procedure, which is only an incidental procedure. On the contrary, this decision is incumbent upon the national trial court, which has to apply the abstract judgement of the ECJ to the specific legal dispute pending before it. With regard to the protection of fundamental rights, it means that in the preliminary reference procedure, only the bases of this protection in Union law are clarified *in abstracto*, however, the individual case-specific implementation remains reserved, based on a strict separation of functions, for the national trial court.

Moreover, the order for reference is an autonomous measure adopted by the procedural judge, and the said measure can neither be enforced and/or prevented by the parties to the proceedings nor can be superseded by an agreement of the parties to the proceedings.

Summa summarum, the preliminary ruling procedure is conceived as *inter iudices* procedure, not as a party-dominated procedure. According to its nature and basic structure, it's not a suitable instrument for pursuing specific interests in protecting individuals, in particular, the specific protection of individual fundamental rights.

6.1.5.3. Procedures, which could, in a modified form, be suitable for an autonomous protection of fundamental rights

Unlike the aforementioned procedures, the following types of procedures, although they are not yet fully suitable for the protection of individual fundamental rights in their present form, however, with relatively minor adjustments, could be moulded into effective instruments for this protection. Together they could constitute a comprehensive system of protection of the fundamental rights in the Union.

6.1.5.3.1. Treaty infringement procedure

The Treaty infringement procedure is, in its present form and specificity, conceived as legal supervision proceedings, which can be initiated by the Commission or a Member State against another Member State. Treaty infringement procedures by natural or legal persons are not provided under the law as it stands at present; the Treaty infringement procedure has no individual rights-protecting character.

This deficit could be eliminated in a fundamental rights-friendly manner by expanding the circle of plaintiffs in this type of procedure to the natural and legal persons, who, as the beneficiaries of the fundamental rights, demand the protection of their own (fundamental) rights. Unlike the institutional plaintiffs, the natural and legal persons must, therefore, prove an interest in bringing an action, namely the need of legal protection, which would result from a violation of their fundamental rights. Thus, the Treaty infringement procedure would retain its character as an institutional procedure, but would also be given the functions of individual action.

As a legal alternative to a widening of the circle of plaintiffs, another solution can be thought of, whereupon natural or legal persons, whose fundamental rights have been violated by the incriminating infringement of Union law by a Member State, could compel the Commission or another Member State to initiate a Treaty infringement procedure against the former State.

The fact that the successful Treaty infringement procedure only leads to a declaratory judgement, whereupon the convicted Member State has to take the necessary measures to comply with the judgment of the Court of Justice (Article 260(1) TFEU; ex-Article 228(1) TEC; ex-Article 143(1) Euratom Treaty), does not conflict with the efficiency of the procedure because the non-compliance with the judgement can lead to another Treaty infringement procedure, within the scope of which the Member State concerned can be urged, by means of a lump sum amount or penalty payment, to comply with its obligations under Union law (Article 260(2) TFEU; ex-Article 228(2) TEC; ex-Article 143(2) Euratom Treaty).

In this context, it seems questionable whether the exhaustion of national remedies can be demanded compellingly (analogous to Article 35(1) ECHR) in the Treaty infringement procedures, which, according to our proposal, could be initiated also by the natural or legal persons due to violations of their fundamental rights guaranteed under the Union law. In our opinion, this should be affirmed, irrespective of the fact that an administrative preliminary procedure must precede the Treaty infringement procedure (Article 258 (1) TFEU; ex-Article 226(1) TEC; ex-Article 141(1) Euratom Treaty): in case of conflict between the requirements of the procedural economy with regard to the individual procedure and the imperative objective to avoid overburdening the Union's jurisdiction, the latter objective should be granted priority.

6.1.5.3.2. Actions for annulment and for failure to act

In contrast to the Treaty infringement procedure, which is directed against a Member State, the actions for annulment and for failure to act are directed against the Union's institutions and bodies. With regard to the circle of defendants, they supplement the Treaty infringement procedure. Problems concerning legal protection are thrown up by the actions for annulment and for failure to act, which are brought by the natural or legal persons, because in these types of actions, the dual threshold of admissibility of direct and individual concern reduces the effect of legal protection. Whereas the criterion of direct concern manifests itself as a consequence of the requirement of an interest in bringing an action and, therewith, is strongly enshrined in the central pillars of the system of legal protection, the criterion of individual concern presents itself as a mere manifestation of procedural expediency and procedural economy and, therefore, can be omitted without any problem for practical reasons.

The objective to comply with the requirements of legal protection would, consequently, demand only minor adjustments to the actions for annulment and for failure to act in order to guarantee a complete and comprehensive protection of fundamental rights: in case of actions brought by natural or legal persons for the annulment of a Union act and/or for the determination of the illegality of the failure to take an action, it would suffice to omit the admissibility criterion of "individual concern" of the plaintiff (Articles 263(4), 265(3) TFEU; ex-Articles 230(4), 232(3) TEC; ex-Articles 146(4), 148(3) Euratom Treaty).

The criterion of "direct concern", which is required in the same provisions and which implies the concern for one's own (fundamental) rights, should, however, be maintained, so that in case of actions brought by natural or legal persons, the proof of an interest in bringing an action would have to be furnished, which would result from the infringement of one's own fundamental rights. Thereby, the basic structure of the actions for annulment and for failure to act is altogether retained.[330]

Attention is deserved by the fact that the successful action for annulment leads to a constitutive judgement (the act concerned is declared "to be void", Article 264(1) TFEU; ex-Article 231(1) TEC; ex-Article 147(1) Euratom Treaty), whereas the complementary action for failure to act, if it is successful, leads to a declaratory judgement (the criticised failure to act is "declared contrary to the Treaties", Article 266(1) TFEU; ex-Article 233(1) TEC; ex-Article 149(1) Euratom

330 The formula "direct and individual concern" used in Article 263(4) TFEU (ex-Article 230(4) TEC; ex-Article 146(4) Euratom Treaty) matches the wording in Article 265(3) TFEU (ex-Article 232(3) TEC; ex-Article 148(3) Euratom Treaty): "to address to that person [= any natural or legal person] any act …". In lieu of these words, it could logically say: "to adopt an act, which is of direct and individual concern to them [= to any natural or legal person]", whereby the words "and individual" would be omitted. In this connection, the amendment in Article 263(4) TFEU in the version of the Lisbon Reform Treaty maybe recollected, which meets our above petitum to a large extent: "…a regulatory act which is of direct concern to them [= to any natural or legal person] and does not entail implementing measures".

Treaty). But this differentiation of the legal consequences has primarily a formal importance, and does not imply any grading of the practical, legally binding effect of the mentioned judgements.

6.1.5.4. Summary appraisal of the "suitability" of the existing types of procedures for the protection of fundamental rights before the institutional Union courts

The preceding overview of the suitability of the most important types of procedures before the institutional Union's courts for the protection of fundamental rights has shown that only the Treaty infringement procedure and the actions for annulment and for failure to act are suitable, in principle, for the protection of fundamental rights. With minor adjustments, they could be moulded into effective instruments for the protection of individual rights and, therewith, for the specific protection of fundamental rights. On the other hand, the actions for damages and the preliminary ruling procedure prove to be, according to their function and structure, unsuitable for an autonomous protection of fundamental rights.

The requisite structural adjustments to the Treaty infringement procedure, as well as to the actions for annulment and for failure to act would be in extending the potential circle of plaintiffs to natural and legal persons in case of an infringement of their own fundamental rights (Treaty infringement procedure) and/or in omitting the requirement of individual concern in the incriminating act or failure to act (actions for annulment and for failure to act). In doing so, a complete system of protection of fundamental rights could be established, which would cover the infringements of fundamental rights in the Union, both by the Member States and the entities and authorities attributable to them (Treaty infringement procedure), as well as by the Union and their institutions and bodies (actions for annulment and for failure to act).

A specific fundamental rights complaint as an instrument to strengthen the protection of individual rights would be unnecessary under these circumstances because the legal disputes on fundamental rights could already be decided in the last-mentioned types of procedures. The establishment of another fundamental rights-protecting procedural institution could, on the contrary, lead to undesirable overlapping of concurrent ways of action, which would be rather harmful than beneficial for the rationality and efficiency of the institutional protection of fundamental rights.

The following reflections on the fundamental rights complaint are, therefore, made only alternatively and hypothetically, should the action and judgement system under Union law be retained in its present incomplete form of legal protection.

6.1.5.5. Introduction of a special fundamental rights complaint

6.1.5.5.1. Preliminary remark

Already the Tindemans report on the European Union of 1975 has advocated the introduction of an – probably inspired by the constitutional complaint under German law – individual complaint against the acts of the Community institutions violating the fundamental rights, but left the contours of such a new legal institute in the dark to a large extent.[331] The question of a specific individual complaint in case of infringements of the fundamental rights guaranteed under Community or Union law is being debated in the legal, as well as in political circles ever since (fundamental rights complaint).[332]

In the following, an attempt is made to elaborate the structural bases of a possible fundamental rights complaint. It should be developed as an instrument for the protection of individual rights; in doing so, the following criteria should be emphasised:

6.1.5.5.2. Subject-matter of an action

The European fundamental rights complaint serves to assert the violations of fundamental rights in the Union. Within the scope of application of the Union law, these rights could be impaired by the acts or omissions by the institutions and bodies of the Union, on the one hand, and by the acts or omissions by the Member States and the entities and authorities attributable to them, on the other hand. Consequently, all the acts or omissions would have to be covered, which are connected to the Union, especially in the implementation, transformation or the ad-

---

331 Tindemans-Bericht, Bulletin of the European Communities, supplement 1/76.

332 Among others, Rudolf Luster/Gero Pfennig/Friedrich Fugmann, Bundesstaat – Europäische Union – Ein Verfassungsentwurf (1988), have advocated the introduction of a constitutional complaint: A Union's constitutional court, which is to be set up, should decide on the "constitutional complaint", which may be filed by any person alleging that one of his fundamental rights in the Union has been infringed by the public authorities (Article 59(1)(a)) of the draft Constitution for Europe). On the other hand, the *Rothley* report by the European Parliament's Committee on Institutional Affairs negated the usefulness of the constitutional complaint, Doc. PE 155/441/final, para 18. For the general discussion on the pros and cons of a communitarian fundamental rights complaint, see: Manfred A. Dauses, Braucht die Europäische Union eine Grundrechtsbeschwerde?, Editorial, in: EuZW 2008, p. 449; Udo Ostermann, Entwicklung und gegenwärtiger Stand der europäischen Grundrechte nach der Rechtsprechung des Europäischen Gerichtshofs sowie des Gerichts erster Instanz, ibid., p. 228 et seqq..

ministrative enforcement of the Union law, even if the Member State concerned has exercised national discretion or has made use of the exceptions to the Union's freedoms.

6.1.5.5.3. Right to bring an action

So as to not let the circle of potential plaintiffs get out of hand, and to avoid overburdening the European jurisdiction, the popular actions by "*quivis ex populo*" should be excluded. Therefore, only those natural or legal persons should be eligible to file applications, whose own rights and, in fact, fundamental rights have been directly affected by the act or omission concerned, but not the persons, who have been affected only economically, thus indirectly, or not at all.

With regard to the criterion of direct concern, Ostermann proposes the formula that the plaintiff must assert that his fundamental rights have been violated presently and directly by the contested measure, that is, a violation of the rights of the plaintiff himself must be given, and the violation must still continue to exist till the date when the fundamental rights complaint is lodged. Moreover, it is to be ensured that the plaintiff objects not just to the legal concern of a third party, which could possibly affect him only in future. However, the requirement of individuality, as it represents the condition for admissibility of the actions for annulment and for failure to act, should not constitute a criterion for the admissibility of the fundamental rights complaint.[333]

6.1.5.5.4. Scope of protection

As already stated, the violations of fundamental rights in the Community or Union could be effected primarily by two categories of subjects:

- by the Union and its institutions and bodies. The violations can result from legislative acts (e.g., regulations, directives), as well as individual measures (e.g., decisions). The failure to enact a Union act also comes into consideration;
- by the Member States and the entities and authorities attributable to them. In this connection, primarily the national acts for the implementation of Union law and/or a failure to take action required under the Union law can be thought of. But even those autonomous acts or omissions of the Member States come into consideration, which are simply contrary to the prior-ranking Union law.

Both the categories of infringements of rights must be covered by the fundamental rights complaint. Thereby, above all, such cases are problematic in which the Un-

333 Udo Ostermann, ibid., p. 232et seq.

ion law is implemented, executed or enforced in any other manner by the national law. Depending on whom to attribute the infringement of the rights, the complaint must be lodged against the Union or rather against the Member State concerned.

6.1.5.5.5. Subsidiarity

To avoid overlapping of concurrent legal recourses and actions, the fundamental rights complaint should – analogously to the provision of Article 35(1) ECHR – strictly be a subsidiary legal remedy.[334] This means that it can be applied only if *in concreto* other procedures are not available or are not pertinent. However, it is not eligible, if the rights-holder, whose fundamental rights have been violated, can and/or could have obtained the remedy of the violation just as well in another way of action. In other words, the fundamental rights complaint is inadmissible due to a lack of interest in bringing an action, if other types of actions, which lead to a similar or a comparable procedural outcome, could be brought by the plaintiff under reasonable conditions.

In this connection, a differentiation needs to be made between the legal remedies available under the Union law and those under the national law:

a) The Union's legal remedies primarily refer to the violations of fundamental rights granted under the Union law by the institutions and bodies of the Union, but can also relate to the violations of fundamental rights by the Member States and their entities and authorities. The following legal remedies are in need of a specific discussion:

- Among other things, the acts and omissions, which are attributable to the Union, and which are contrary to the fundamental rights, could be objected to within the scope of the Union's actions for annulment and for failure to act. Consequently, these actions also perform the functions of a fundamental rights complaint to some extent.[335] Their successful outcome leads to the annulment of the challenged act and/or to the determination of an obligation to act on the part of the defendant institution or the defendant body. But, therewith, an interest in bringing an action becomes inapplicable for a subsequent special fundamental rights complaint; the latter becomes devoid of purpose.
- However, no subsidiarity relationship of the fundamental rights complaint vis-à-vis the Union's actions for damages should be assumed, because the latter have an entirely different subject-matter and a different objective than

334 Norbert Reich, Zur Notwendigkeit einer Europäischen Grundrechtsbeschwerde, in: ZRP 2000, p. 375, 378.

335 Christian Calliess, Kohärenz und Konvergenz beim europäischen Individualrechtsschutz. Der Zugang zum Gericht im Lichte des Grundrechts auf effektiven Rechtsschutz, in: NJW 2002, p. 3577, 3581.

the fundamental rights complaint: legally binding acts cannot be annulled by means of the action for damages, existing violations of fundamental rights cannot be redressed; a review as to what extent the fundamental rights were violated, takes place only incidentally. Even a possible rehabilitation interest of the plaintiff can be considered just as little in this procedure as a possible interest in a defence against imminent violations of fundamental rights in future. Consequently, the sheer possibility to get compensation for damages does not conflict with the admissibility of the fundamental rights complaint, because even in case of a success of an action for damages, an interest in bringing an action for a fundamental rights complaint can continue to exist.

- A subsidiarity relationship of the fundamental rights complaint vis-à-vis the Treaty infringement procedure is to be assumed just as little in its present form. The latter refers to the infringements of Union law, and also the violations of the Union's fundamental rights, by the Member States and the entities and authorities attributable to them. However, the procedure is purely an institutional process, which can be initiated and carried out only by the Commission or a Member State; a participation of private parties in this procedure is not envisaged. This type of action is, therefore, not a procedure, whose precedence could be a precondition for the admissibility of the fundamental rights complaint.
- Finally, the fundamental rights complaint can also not be assessed as subsidiary to the preliminary ruling procedure. The latter serves as an interlocutory procedure in a legal dispute pending before a Member State court only for the abstract, even if case-specific, review of validity and interpretation of the Union law, and not for the specific decision on the dispute, which is reserved for the national trial court. Therefore, specific violations of fundamental rights cannot be decided in the preliminary ruling procedure itself. Add to this the fact that the parties to the main proceedings cannot have any influence on the initiation and execution of a preliminary ruling procedure. For the aforementioned reasons, the fundamental rights complaint cannot be made contingent upon that a preliminary ruling procedure should precede it.

b) A subsidiarity relationship can exist not only between the fundamental rights complaint and any other Union procedure, but also between the fundamental rights complaint and a procedure, which is aimed at the same objective, before a Member State court. Even in such a case, the fundamental rights complaint can be lodged only after the parallel action was executed before the Member State court without any success.[336]

- Such priority legal remedies under the national law, the prior exhaustion of which would have to be looked upon as a precondition for the admissibility of the fundamental rights complaint, refer, without exception, to violations of the Union's fundamental rights by the Member States and their entities and authorities. To what extent such legal remedies must be taken in advance *in concreto*, depends on the respective type of the proceedings.
- Basically, it can be said that the exhaustion of the national remedies can only mean the exhaustion of legal remedies by the specialised courts. On the other hand, applying for specific legal remedies available under the constitution, such as e.g., the constitutional complaint under German law (Article 93(1)(4a) Basic Law (GG)), would not be any precondition for the admissibility of the fundamental rights complaint, if only the violation of the national fundamental rights is decided by the national remedies.[337]
- The objection that the ECJ must, in case of obligatory exhaustion of national remedies, also review and apply the Member State law, does not conflict with the correct application of the "*local remedies rule*", because the ECJ is obligated, in other types of actions as well, such as e.g., the Treaty infringement procedure, to rely upon the national law as the precondition for the correct assessment of the Union law. The strict separation between the Union and the Member State legal order is, therefore, not an irreversible postulate. In practical application to the fundamental rights complaint, it means that the ECJ has to familiarise itself with the legal systems of the Member States, at least insofar as it helps in examining whether the subsidiarity of the fundamental rights complaint was respected.

Admittedly, the subsidiarity rule is effective only with regard to the procedures, which are not absolutely futile. For instance, futile would be an (inadmissible) individual action for annulment directed against a genuine normative act adopted by legislative procedure and/or an (inadmissible) individual action for failure to act aimed at the enactment of a genuine normative act. From the general principle of efficiency, it follows that the exhaustion of legal remedies, which do not offer any reasonable chance of success, cannot be any precondition for the admissibility of the fundamental rights complaint.

---

336 Parallels to Article 35(1) ECHR are quite obvious here, according to which the European Court of Human Rights can deal with a matter only "after exhaustion of all domestic remedies" ("*local remedies rule*").

337 Udo Ostermann, ibid., p. 233.

In practice, one could expect from the plaintiff that he also states in his complaint, what other legal remedies he has taken beforehand, without success, and/ or that *in concreto* no other legal remedy was available with a reasonable chance of success.

6.1.5.5.6. Substantive jurisdiction of the ECJ

In this connection, the question of the jurisdiction *ratione materiae* (substantive jurisdiction) of the Court adjudicating on the complaint in the relationship between the ECJ and the GC is posed: because of the constitutional dimension of the fundamental rights complaint, it seems appropriate to abstain from a two-stage appeal process (first instance: GC; appeal procedure: ECJ), and to declare the ECJ, in its capacity as the constitutional court of the Union, as having jurisdiction in the first and only instance.

On the other hand, the ECJ has the appellate jurisdiction for the procedures before the GC. Therewith, on the one hand, it would have jurisdiction, as the court of the first instance, for the fundamental rights complaints, on the other hand, it would be the court of appeal for other individual actions in which the violations of fundamental rights could be challenged. This dual jurisdiction could, if the procedures are pending before the ECJ and the GC at the same time, justify a joining of the cases as useful from the point of view of the procedural economy. Then, the ECJ would decide with one and the same judgement on the fundamental rights complaint, as well as on the appeal. In such a case, the principle of procedural subordination of the fundamental rights complaint would step back in favour of a procedural coincidence.

6.1.5.5.7. Legal effects of a judgement to be granted

In order to achieve an effective protection of fundamental rights, the decision on the fundamental rights complaint cannot be restricted to an abstract judgement for the mere determination of the substance of fundamental rights protected under the Union law, as is the case, for instance, in the preliminary ruling procedure. Rather, the fundamental rights complaint must be able to be formulated case-specific and likewise to be decided case-specific. In other words, this complaint should be conceived and shaped as a direct action. With regard to the violations of fundamental rights in the Member States, this petitum implies that, if need be, even the national law must be reviewed for its compatibility with the fundamental rights of the Union.

The effects of the complaint usually find expression in the wording of the judgement. Thereby, differentiation can be made between the violations of fundamental rights by the Union's institutions and bodies, on the one hand, and by the

Member States and the entities and authorities attributable to them, on the other hand. In both cases, however, the regime should be modelled on the existing system of action and judgement in the Union and, in fact, as follow:

- in case of violations of the fundamental rights by the Union's institutions and bodies, *mutatis mutandis,* the wording of the judgment upholding the claim in the actions of annulment and for failure to act should be adopted (i.e., constitutive declaration of annulment of the fundamental rights-violating act and/or determination of the violation of the fundamental rights caused by the incriminating omission, in conjunction with a corresponding obligation of the defendant to take the measures to comply with the judgement);
- in case of violations of the fundamental rights by the Member States and the entities and authorities attributable to them, *mutatis mutandis,* the wording of the judgement upholding the claim in the Treaty infringement procedure should be adopted (i.e., determination of the violation of the fundamental rights caused by the incriminating act or omission, in conjunction with a corresponding obligation of the defendant to take the measures to comply with the judgement).

With regard to the obligation to comply with a declaratory judgement, attention should be paid that the content of this obligation can, in fact, be partly concretised already in the declaratory judgement itself. However, the obligation to comply is finally incumbent upon the defendant on his own responsibility.

7. Conclusion

According to their historical emergence and development, the fundamental rights in the Community and/or the Union are primarily judge-made law; they are based on case-specific judicature of the ECJ, from which, gradually, a consistent fundamental rights doctrine developed, whereupon, corresponding to the economic emphasis of the EC/EU, the fundamental economic rights are in the limelight. Already before the codified commitment to these rights in Article 6(2) TEU (version of the Maastricht Treaty), the ECJ had inferred the fundamental rights as general principles of the Community law from the sources of the knowledge of law given in the European Convention for the Protection of Human Rights and Fundamental Freedoms, and – by way of an evaluative comparison of laws – in the constitutional traditions common to the Member States. With the proclamation of the Charter of Fundamental Rights of the European Union of 7.12.2000, this act has come along as another *fons cognoscendi*. It has, since the Lisbon Reform Treaty is in force, become the first written and legally binding catalogue of fundamental rights of the European Union. Therewith, although it is not a formal part of the reformed Union Treaty, however, with reference to Article 6(1) TEU (new version), it is directly applicable substantive Union law.

So where does the benefit of a legally binding codification lie? The clear deficits, which resulted in the past from the missing written form of the binding fundamental rights norms, lie in the area of legal clarity and legal certainty and the obstacles connected therewith for the predictability and calculability of the relevant law. They extend to the elements of protection, scope of application and restrictions on fundamental rights. Above all, the restrictive clauses, which are routinely asserted by the ECJ, concerning the "objectives of general interest pursued by the Community" give rise to criticism. They leave a wide scope of discretion, which cannot always be adequately curtailed even by the limits of restrictions, such as the principle of proportionality and the guarantee of the substance.

The provisos of "general interest" are surely justified, but should follow clear, specifically formulated rules. The case-law of the ECJ lacks these not infrequently. It gives the impression that the ECJ sees itself primarily as the "driving force of European integration" and, in case of doubt, grants priority to the interests of the Community over those of the fundamental rights-holders; in doing so, the Community objectives are not really weighed against the interests in protecting individuals. This shortcoming could now be eliminated by the bindingly applicable Charter of Fundamental Rights. The achieved fundamental rights standard of the Union could be conspicuously documented thereby; the individuals could be sure of the rights entitled to them.

With the mere commitment to fundamental rights alone, however, the protection of fundamental rights cannot be sufficiently guaranteed at the Union level. Just as important are efficient options of legal remedies, which are available to the individual against infringements of the fundamental rights. The European Charter of Fundamental Rights does not enshrine – unlike the European Convention on Human Rights – any inherent provisions concerning the legal protection and jurisdiction, so that, in case of violations of fundamental rights guaranteed by the Union, only the general legal-protection provisions of the Union Treaties apply. Do these suffice or are they in need of an adjustment and supplementation?

With the constitutional complaint (Article 93(1)(4)(a) GG), the German Basic Law opens up the possibility for the citizens to effectively enforce their fundamental rights. The constitutional complaint supplements the "subconstitutionally" guaranteed judicial protection of individual rights, and is the only way by which the individual can – after the exhaustion of the non-constitutional remedies– immediately bring an action before the Federal Constitutional Court. In Union law, however, unlike in the German legal order, the fundamental rights beneficiaries do not have any corresponding special procedural instrument at their disposal. On the other hand, the existing instruments for the protection of fundamental rights do not suffice to ensure a complete protection of individual rights.

In order to find remedies, first of all, the scope of the existing possibilities of actions should be exhausted by opening the requirements for access to these procedures. Thereby, primarily the access to the Union's judicature must be made easier for the natural and legal persons. In this regard, in view of the violations of the Union's fundamental rights by the Member States, it is recommended to adapt the Treaty infringement procedure, and in view of such violations by the Union, to adapt the actions for annulment and for failure to act to the fundamental rights-holders' need for protection. The former type of action (Articles 258-260 TFEU) should be restructured in such a way that even the natural and legal persons can bring actions (and not just, as it has been the case until now, the European Commission and the Member States). On the other hand, the actions for annulment and for failure to act (Articles 263-266 TFEU) should be modified in such a manner that the natural and legal persons could use them, whenever the questionable act or omission affects them directly, but, nevertheless, not necessarily individually.

As for the rest, the Union system of legal protection could remain unchanged. The introduction of a specific fundamental rights complaint of the Union is not advocated. No need is given under the above preconditions for such a new procedural instrument, which, moreover, must strictly be subsidiary to the other legal remedies with equal or similar objectives.

Bibliography

In this list of literature, the most important references to the literature, which have been cited in this study, were included. In case of citations from books, basically only the miscellany concerned, and not the respective individual contributions, has been mentioned. However, the latter have been listed in the footnotes together with the bibliographic references to the miscellany in which they have been published.

Alber, Siegbert, Die Selbstbindung der europäischen Organe an die Europäische Charta der Grundrechte, EuGRZ 2001, p. 349

Alber, Siegbert/ Widmaier, Ulrich, Die EU-Charta der Grundrechte und ihre Auswirkungen auf die Rechtsprechung. Zu den Beziehungen zwischen EuGH und EGMR, EuGRZ 2000, p. 497

von Arnim, Dorothee, Der Standort der EU-Grundrechtecharta in der Grundrechtsarchitektur Europas, Dissertation, Würzburg 2006

Blank, Michael, Soziale Grundrechte in der Europäischen Grundrechtecharta, 2002

Bleckmann, Albert, Staatsrecht II – Die Grundrechte, 3rd edition 1989

Bleckmann, Albert, Die Rechtsquellen des Europäischen Gemeinschaftsrechts, NVwZ 1993, p. 824

Bleckmann, Albert/Pieper, Stefan Ulrich, Rechtsquellen, in: Manfred A. Dauses (Hrsg.), Handbuch des EU-Wirtschaftsrechts, loose-leaf binder, Vol. I, B.I.

Brigola, Alexander, Das System der EG-Grundfreiheiten: Vom Diskriminierungsverbot zum spezifischen Beschränkungsverbot, Dissertation, Erlangen-Nürnberg 2004

Busse, Christian, Eine kritische Würdigung der Präambel der Europäischen Grundrechtecharta, EuGRZ 2002, p. 559

Calliess, Christian, Die Charta der Grundrechte der Europäischen Union – Fragen der Konzeption, Kompetenz und Verbindlichkeit, EuZW 2001, p. 261

Calliess, Christian, Kohärenz und Konvergenz beim europäischen Individualrechtsschutz. Der Zugang zum Gericht im Lichte des Grundrechts auf effektiven Rechtsschutz, NJW 2002, p. 3577

Calliess, Christian/Ruffert, Matthias (Hrsg.), EUV/EGV. Das Verfassungsrecht der Europäischen Union mit Europäischer Grundrechtecharta, Commentary, 3rd edition, 2007

Chwolik-Lanfermann, Ellen, Braucht die Europäische Union einen Grundrechtskatalog?, ZRP 1995, p. 126

Däubler-Gmelin, Herta, Eine europäische Charta der Grundrechte – Beitrag zur gemeinsamen Identität, EuZW 2000, p. 1

Daig, Hans-Wolfram, Nichtigkeits- und Untätigkeitsklagen im Recht der Europäischen Gemeinschaften – unter besonderer Berücksichtigung der Rechtsprechung des Gerichtshofs der Europäischen Gemeinschaften und der Schlussanträge der Generalanwälte, 1985

Dauses, Manfred A., Der Schutz der Grundrechte in der Europäischen Gemeinschaft, JÖR, Vol. 31, 1982, p. 1

Dauses, Manfred A., The Protection of Fundamental Rights in the Community Legal Order, ELR 1985, p. 398

Dauses, Manfred A., Empfiehlt es sich, das System des Rechtsschutzes und der Gerichtsbarkeit in der Europäischen Gemeinschaft, insbesondere die Aufgaben der Gemeinschaftsgerichte und der nationalen Gerichte, weiterzuentwickeln?, Gutachten zum 60. Deutschen Juristentag Münster 1994

Dauses, Manfred A., Das Vorabentscheidungsverfahren nach Artikel 177 EG-Vertrag, 2nd edition 1995

Dauses, Manfred A., Grundrechte als Elemente einer Verfassungsordnung der Europäischen Union, in: Winfried Böttcher (Hrsg.), Europäische Perspektiven, 2002, p. 29

Dauses, Manfred A., Braucht die Europäische Union eine Grundrechtsbeschwerde?, EuZW 2008, p. 449

Dauses, Manfred A. (Hrsg.), Handbuch des EU-Wirtschaftsrechts, 2 volumes, loose-leaf binder, 26th amending supplement, as of June 2010

de Búrca, Gráinne, The Drafting of the European Union Charter of Fundamental Rights, ELR 2001, p. 126

Denninger, Erhard, Menschenrechte und Staatsaufgaben – ein europäisches Thema, JZ 1996, p. 585

Eisner, Carolin, Die Schrankenregelung der Grundrechtecharta der Europäischen Union: Gefahr oder Fortschritt für den Grundrechtsschutz in Europa?, 2005

Everling, Ulrich, Das Vorabentscheidungsverfahren vor dem Gerichtshof der Europäischen Gemeinschaften, 1986

Everling, Ulrich, Brauchen wir „Solange III"?, EuR 1990, p. 195

Feger, Dieter, Die Grundrechte im Recht der Europäischen Gemeinschaften – Bestand und Entwicklung, 1984

Feger, Dieter, Die Normsetzung auf dem Gebiet der Grundrechte in den Europäischen Gemeinschaften – Der Europäische Gerichtshof (EuGH) als Rechtsetzungsorgan, DÖV 1987, p. 322

Gersdorf, Hubertus, Funktionen der Gemeinschaftsgrundrechte im Lichte des Solange II-Beschlusses des Bundesverfassungsgerichts, AöR 1994, p. 400

Golsong, Heribert, Nochmals: zur Frage des Beitritts der Europäischen Gemeinschaften zur Europäischen Menschenrechtskonvention, EuGRZ 1979, p. 70

Grabenwarter, Christoph, Die Charta der Grundrechte für die Europäische Union, DVB1 2001, p. 1.

Grabenwarter, Christoph, Auf dem Weg in die Grundrechtsgemeinschaft?, EuGRZ 2004, p. 563

Grabitz, Eberhard/ Hilf, Meinhard (Hrsg.), Das Recht der Europäischen Union, Commentary, 5 volumes, loose-leaf binder, 32nd amending supplement, as of April 2007

von der Groeben, Hans/Thiesing, Jochen/ Ehlermann, Claus-Dieter (Hrsg.), Commentary on EU/EC Treaty, 4 volumes, 5th edition, 1997

von der Groeben, Hans/Schwarze, Jürgen (Hrsg.), Vertrag über die Europäische Union und Vertrag zur Gründung der Europäischen Gemeinschaft, Commentary, 4 volumes, 6th edition, 2004

Hilf, Meinhard, Solange II: Wie lange noch Solange?, EuGRZ 1987, p. 1

Hilf, Meinhard, Ein Grundrechtskatalog für die Europäische Gemeinschaft, EuR 1991, p. 19

Hoffmann, Gunter M., Grundrechte in Europa – braucht Europa einen Grundrechtskatalog?, 1995

Iber, Andrea, Der Status der Grundrechtscharta im Gemeinschaftsrecht – Derzeitige Verbindlichkeit und Zukunftsperspektiven der Charta – insbesondere im Verfassungskonvent, ZEuS 2002, p. 483

Ipsen, Hans Peter, Europäisches Gemeinschaftsrecht, 1972

Jarass, Hans D., EU-Grundrechte, 2005

Jellinek, Georg, Allgemeine Staatslehre, 3rd edition, 1914, reprint 1966

Kenntner, Markus, Die Schrankenbestimmungen der EU-Grundrechtecharta – Grundrechte ohne Schutzwirkung?, ZRP 2000, p. 423

Kischel, Uwe, Die Kontrolle der Verhältnismäßigkeit durch den Europäischen Gerichtshof, EuR 2000, p. 380

Knecht, Matthias H., Die Charta der Grundrechte der Europäischen Union: Eine Würdigung der Entstehung und rechtsvergleichende grundrechtsdogmatische Analyse, 2005

Commission of the European Communities, Communication from the Commission on the legal nature of the Charter of fundamental rights of the European Union, Brussels, 11.10.2000, COM (2000) 644 final

Kühling, Jürgen, Grundrechtskontrolle durch den EuGH: Kommunikationsfreiheit und Pluralismussicherung im Gemeinschaftsrecht, EuGRZ 1997, p. 296
Lecheler, Helmut, Der Europäische Gerichtshof und die allgemeinen Rechtsgrundsätze, 1971
Lenz, Carl Otto/Borchhardt, Klaus-Dieter (Hrsg.), EU- und EG-Vertrag, Kommentar zu dem Vertrag über die Europäische Union und zu dem Vertrag zur Gründung der Europäischen Gemeinschaft, 4th edition, 2006
Lindner, Josef Franz, Grundrechtsschutz gegen gemeinschaftliche Öffnungsklauseln – zugleich ein Beitrag zum Anwendungsbereich der EU-Grundrechte, EuZW 2007, p. 71
Magiera, Siegfried, Die Grundrechtecharta der Europäischen Union, DÖV 2000, p. 1017
Mahlmann, Matthias, Die Grundrechtecharta der Europäischen Union, ZEuS 2000, p. 419
Merten, Detlef/Papier, Hans-Jürgen, Handbuch der Grundrechte, 2004
Meyer, Jürgen (Hrsg.), Die Charta der Grundrechte der Europäischen Union – Berichte und Dokumentation, 2001
Meyer, Jürgen (Hrsg.), Kommentar zur Charta der Grundrechte der Europäischen Union, 1st edition, 2003, 2nd edition, 2006
Meyer, Jürgen/Engels, Markus, Aufnahme von sozialen Grundrechten in die Europäische Grundrechtecharta?, ZRP 2000, p. 368
von Milczewski, Christine, Der grundrechtliche Schutz des Eigentums im Europäischen Gemeinschaftsrecht, 1994
Nettesheim, Martin, Grundrechtliche Prüfdichte durch den EuGH, EuZW 1995, p. 106
Nettesheim, Martin, Die Charta der Grundrechte der Europäischen Union: Eine verfassungstheoretische Kritik, Integration 2002, p. 35
Ostermann, Udo, Entwicklung und gegenwärtiger Stand der europäischen Grundrechte nach der Rechtsprechung des Europäischen Gerichtshofs sowie des Gerichts erster Instanz, Dissertation, Erlangen-Nürnberg 2008
Anon., Explanations relating to the Charter of Fundamental Rights of 14.12.2007, OJ. 2007, C 303/17
Pache, Eckhardt, Die Europäische Grundrechtscharta – ein Rückschritt für den Grundrechtsschutz in Europa?, EuR 2001, p. 475
Pauly, Walter, Strukturfragen des unionsrechtlichen Grundrechtsschutzes, EuR 1998, p. 242
Pernice, Ingolf, Grundrechtsgehalte im europäischen Gemeinschaftsrecht – Ein Beitrag zum gemeinschaftsimmanenten Grundrechtsschutz durch den Europäischen Gerichtshof, 1979

Pernice, Ingolf, Gemeinschaftsverfassung und Grundrechtsschutz – Grundlagen, Bestand, Perspektiven, NJW 1990, p. 2409
Pernice, Ingolf, Eine Grundrechte-Charta für die Europäische Union, DVBl. 2000, p. 847
Pescatore, Pierre, Bestand und Bedeutung der Grundrechte im Recht der Europäischen Gemeinschaften, EuR 1979, p. 1
Philippi, Nina, Die Charta der Grundrechte der Europäischen Union, 2002
Radbruch, Gustav, Gesetzliches Unrecht und übergesetzliches Recht, SJZ 1946, p. 105
Reich, Norbert, Zur Notwendigkeit einer Europäischen Grundrechtsbeschwerde, ZRP 2000, p. 375
Rengeling, Hans-Werner, Grundrechtsschutz in der Europäischen Gemeinschaft, 1993
Rengeling, Hans-Werner/Szczekalla, Peter, Grundrechte in der Europäischen Union – Charta der Grundrechte und allgemeine Rechtsgrundsätze, 2004
Ruffert, Matthias, Die Mitgliedstaaten der Europäischen Gemeinschaft als Verpflichtete der Gemeinschaftsgrundrechte, EuGRZ 1995, p. 518
Scheuing, Dieter, Zur Grundrechtsbindung der EU-Mitgliedstaaten, EuR 2005, p. 162
Schildknecht, Urs, Grundrechtsschranken in der Europäischen Gemeinschaft, 2000
Schilling, Theodor, Bestand und allgemeine Lehren der bürgerschützenden allgemeinen Rechtsgrundsätze des Gemeinschaftsrechts, EuGRZ 2000, p. 3
Schmittmann, Georg J., Rechte und Grundsätze in der Grundrechtecharta, 2007
Schmitz, Thomas, Die Grundrechtecharta als Teil der Verfassung der Europäischen Union, EuR 2004, p. 691
Scholz, Rupert, Wie lange bis „Solange III"?, NJW 1990, p. 941
Schwarze, Jürgen, Europäisches Verwaltungsrecht – Entstehung und Entwicklung im Rahmen der Europäischen Gemeinschaft, 2 volumes, 1988
Stern, Klaus/Tettinger, Peter (Hrsg.), Kölner Gemeinschaftskommentar zur Europäischen Grundrechte-Charta, 2006
Streinz, Rudolf, Bundesverfassungsgerichtlicher Grundrechtsschutz und Europäisches Gemeinschaftsrecht, 1989
Streinz, Rudolf (Hrsg.), EUV/EGV, Vertrag über die Europäische Union und Vertrag zur Gründung der Europäischen Gemeinschaft, 2003
Tettinger, Peter J., Die Charta der Grundrechte der Europäischen Union, NJW 2001, p. 1010
Thiel, Jürgen Michael, Europa 1992: Grundrechtlicher Eigentumsschutz im EG-Recht, JuS 1991, p. 274

Voß, Reimer, Erfahrungen und Probleme bei der Anwendung des Vorabentscheidungsverfahrens nach Artikel 177 EWGV, EuR 1986, p. 95

Weber, Albrecht, Die Europäische Grundrechtscharta – auf dem Weg zu einer europäischen Verfassung, NJW 2000, p. 537

Weber, Albrecht, Charta der Grundrechte der Europäischen Union, 2002

Zuleeg, Manfred, Zum Verhältnis nationaler und europäischer Grundrechte, Funktionen einer EU-Charta der Grundrechte, EuGRZ 2000, p. 511